The Extraordinary Madness of Banks and the Extreme Folly of Governments

Chris Skinner #GFC

Book 5 of The Complete Banker series – new edition

By Chris Skinner

The
**Complete
Banker**

First published 2010 by Balatro Limited, 98 Westbury Lane, Buckhursthill, IG9 5PW, UK . This revised edition published 2011.

ISBN 978-1-907720-36-9

Edited and produced by Searching Finance Ltd, 8 Whitehall Road, London W7 2JE, UK. Tel: +44 (0) 7885 441682; email: enquiries@searchingfinance.com; web: www.searchingfinance.com

The Extraordinary Madness of Banks and the Extreme Folly of Governments

Chris Skinner #GFC

Book 5 of The Complete Banker series – new edition

By Chris Skinner

The
Complete
Banker

About Chris Skinner

Chris has been providing independent, expert commentary on the key developments in banking for over a decade in his role as Chief Executive of Balatro and Chairman of the Financial Services Club. In particular, he has been writing for various media, such as the Banker Magazine, since 2004 and is a key commentator on banking for prime time news channels including the BBC, Sky and Bloomberg. Prior to creating his independent entities, Chris had key roles at management and board levels covering insurance, retail and investment banking across a range of consulting and technology firms.

Chris has worked worldwide delivering advice, keynote speeches, presentations and workshops to many banks and vendors worldwide, including Accenture, American Express, ANZ, Bank of America, Bank of Baroda, Cisco, Hewlett Packard, Liberty Bank, Lloyds TSB, McKinsey, Merrill Lynch, Microsoft, National Australia Bank, Nationwide Building Society, NCR, TATA, the National Bank of Kuwait, the Union Bank of the Philippines, Wachovia Bank, Washington Mutual, and many others.

About the Financial Services Club

The Financial Services Club is a unique service aimed at senior executives and decision makers from banks, insurance companies, technology firms, consultancies ... in fact, any firm that is interested in understanding and planning for the future operating environment for the financial services markets.

The Financial Services Club bridges the gap between today and tomorrow. It allows you to network with hundreds of professionals all sharing a common interest in the future of the industry. The Club hosts over 50 events a year, in a number of different European countries, with keynote speakers and luminaries from the industry airing their views on the future of financial services. Our illustrious speaker list is targeted to cover all aspects of the industry from practitioners to legislators to futurists.

For more information, go to http://www.fsclub.co.uk

Contents

*The Extraordinary Madness of Banks and the
Extreme Folly of Governments*

Preface

In this fifth book in the Complete Banker series, I struggled to find a title. After all, what do you call a book about the financial crisis, when there are so many books out there already. *Too Big to Fail, the Storm, 13 Bankers, the Big Short* ... the list goes on. In fact, it's got to the stage that yet another book about the financial crisis would just be boring.

So this is not a book about the crisis. This book is about the outcome.

It tracks the markets from the day that Lehman Brothers collapsed, and before with Northern Rock, through the reactions of policymakers, politicians, regulators and markets. It shows where the weaknesses were in hindsight, and where the pitfalls may be in foresight.

It tries to give the reader a chance to absorb and understand the key movements that created the crisis, and the explanation of why banks, bonuses and bosses are still at the trough feeding and greeding their way through the issues faced.

I use these terms loosely, because one title was going to be *Bulls, Bears, Pigs and Fat Cats*. One of the biggest issues in this crisis has been the reaction of bankers afterwards, with major bonus payments in 2009 and 2010. This has been the biggest issue because, whilst the rest of the world was suffering recession, bankers were still making money and the banks that made these payments were often bailed out by taxpayers. That caused fury and anger, but has still to find a resolution.

Equally, I thought about calling this book *Another Bank Hits the Wall*, but thought it too cryptic. It was a little pun on the Pink Floyd classic track 'The Wall', and the fact that around 500 banks worldwide have hit the wall since this crisis hit would have been appropriate as a title.

Another title was *Crisis? What Crisis?* Another old track – this was the title of a Supertramp album back in 1975 – and again, very appropriate as many would think that after trillions of dollars of quantitative easing and bailouts, the financial markets would show some sort of contrition or humility. Nope. Financial markets naturally behave as though there was never an issue, and they do this purposefully because financial markets act like a jungle where only the most adaptable survive.

Just look at the crisis in the Eurozone with Greece soon followed by Ireland, then Italy and Spain, into a maelstrom of debt funding issues. Interestingly, much of this has nothing to do with a sovereign debt crisis, as widely reported. Instead, it's a crisis of leadership, with all the markets betting the Eurozone will crash unless and until the European Central Bank steps in to sort out the mess through direct central bank funding.

Something which, at the time of writing, the Germans have resisted but which appears to be inevitable.

So the markets are mad, and right now, they're mad with the Europeans.

Tomorrow, who knows?

So that's why I finally settled upon *The Extraordinary Madness of Bankers and the Extreme Folly of Governments* as the title of this book. This is not meant to insult banks and bankers, many of whom are nice people. You may not realise it, but of the millions of people working in banks worldwide, only 0.1% are the bonus boys and girls. That means that 99.9% are just honest-to-goodness branch workers, managers, call centre customer service representatives and similar administrative workers. These folks should not receive the ire and irritation of the public as they had nothing to do with creating the financial crisis.

Equally, you probably shouldn't be annoyed with the 0.1% who make the multimillion dollar bonuses. After all, these folks are rewarded for creating and taking risks with money. That's why they get those bonuses, as the payment is made for generating profits.

Nope, the real irritation should be with the management who allowed the crisis to happen, and that's not just bank management but governance all round. From the policymaking economists to the lack of regulating regulators, the issues are a muddle of many; and their resolution will take years.

So that's what this book is all about, and the title is based upon a classic tale from times of old: *Extraordinary Popular Delusions & the Madness of Crowds,* by Charles Mackay. This is a book written way back in the 19th century, and explains how crowds invest, buy and sell based upon popular mania. It has nothing to do with market forces, but is all based upon market fads. That's what happened here: the market created a fad for wrapping up risk in untested derivatives that proved to be riskier than any before.

This book will show you how it all happened, and is the fifth in our Complete Banker series. If you want to really understand the banking system, then the other books will provide you with a comprehensive knowledge.

Have fun and enjoy the read,

Chris

PS: The articles herein have been selected from white papers, presentations and other research I have undertaken, and from my regular Financial Services Club blog postings at www.thefinanser. com; for more information on the Financial Services Club, go to http://www.fsclub.co.uk

.

Chapter 1 Anatomy of the crisis

Introduction

The credit crisis origins began in the late 1990s, when JPMorgan's investment team came up with the idea of a new product called the Credit Default Swap (CDS). Within a decade, these products had become all-encompassing in the global financial markets, as they mitigated risk. Many other complex financial products were spawned by CDS, including Collateralised Debt Obligations (CDO) and Mortgage Backed Securities (MBS), along with a large number of other Special Purpose Vehicles (SPV). OK, so I've already introduced a whole range of acronyms that may confuse and bewilder, but that's what happened in this crisis. Investment markets created lots of new bewildering and confusing products that supposedly eradicated risks but instead created the riskiest set of financial instruments ever seen. One of the key things here, however, is that it was all known. Many people saw the risks in these instruments. The failure therefore is that no-one cried out: "it's the Emperor's new clothes". No-one bothered to point out that there was nothing there but a house of risky cards that would eventually fall. Of course, we would shout out today, but it's so much easier in hindsight. So here's the hindsight ...

The similarities between banks and landmines (2011)

Last night I was presenting to the MAG-net group. MAG-net is the networking group in the City for the Mines Advisory Group, MAG, a charity supported by the Financial Services Club and others that clears areas of mines so that schools, villages and life can continue as it should in post-war territories.

They invited me to speak about anything I wanted, and so I created a new presentation about the similarities between banks and landmines. The presentation developed around the idea of banks being mines that explode in economic terms, in a similar way in which landmines explode and blow away people and animals in the real world.

My premise was that just as landmines blow the legs away from humans, banks blow the legs off economies.

It's obviously the case that this is true today, what with the Lehmans collapse with credit default swaps creating the first financial crisis; and now sovereign debt in the Eurozone is developing the second.

How can such economic landmines exist in a world where we should have cleared them by now? They exist because we allow innovation in financial instruments in an unregulated form. That innovation is all around derivatives of derivatives. Untried and untested weapons of financial destruction are being created every day and planted as hidden potentially unexploded bombs across the financial system.

This has been well documented in many books, with F.I.A.S.C.O. cited by many as a great illustration of the issues in a storybook form or, if you prefer the academic version, 'Infectious Greed', gives you the lowdown.

These two books by Frank Partnoy document the issues of derivatives, which are both good and bad.

They are good in creating leveraged risk which allows commerce to become more capable. They are good in hedging risk, allowing trades to take place that otherwise could not. They are good in bringing together mixed asset classes, so that previously unrelated goods and services can now be traded together. They are good in offsetting future uncertainty, which is why they are used.

They are bad because they are so complex, most traders don't understand them. They are bad because they are called 'exotics', and are so exotic that they can explode. They are bad because they allow firms, such as Goldman Sachs, to create a massively web of interlinkage between risk that ensures those in their world can have huge exposures whilst Goldman itself avoid such loss. They are bad because they allow debt to be leveraged so greatly that it becomes unmanageable.

All of the latter are the landmines of economies, and are no better demonstrated than by Lehmans collapse and Europe's sovereign debt crisis. Again, derivatives were used to package sovereign debt in the same way as mortgage debt, and has created this second loss of confidence in the European economies

Now don't think I'm Goldman bashing because they are the most effective bulge bracket player in the world's markets in creating risk and therefore alpha returns. That's why their clients use them. However, they are also the most effective institutions in the world's markets in creating risks that can explode in the face of their clients. That's why they sell 'crap' to their customers (by their own admittance) and are happy to do it.

And the only positive note is that we can save human limbs by clearing landmines using mice to sniff the mines out.

Let's get some more mice in the financial markets.

Unimaginable and unmanageable risks, or total transparency and control? (2011)

Just sat through a day of academic debate about the financial crisis and how much technology was to blame. We've had these blame games many times in the past, usually to try to point a finger at an individual like Greenspan or Brown, so taking the finger to point to an inanimate pile of metal processors was going to prove interesting I thought.

The real point of the whole day was to point to the origins of the crisis – the rich and diverse world of derivatives – and to say that the complexity of quantum analytics that drove us down the spiral of debt was due to the systems handling our formulas in such a way that it made it look like risk was managed ... but it wasn't.

In other words, the computers messed up. One speaker pointed out that risk was hidden because regulators focused upon individual financial institutions instead of systemic risks across the industry. Another talked about the origins of the Black-Scholes system, and said that "it wasn't technologists who caused the crisis, but physicists". Another mooted the scale of computing, and how complex analytics had moved us into grids, data centres and clouds, that provided unlimited processing and scalability. Hence, what could never have been mapped, simulated or contemplated before could now just be modelled and deployed overnight.

Whatever your view, systems are a contributor to this crisis, but it's not the systems that caused it but the people who programmed them. So here's my potted view of how technology exacerbated the crisis and what will happen next ...

The Black-Scholes formula meant that if you were buying or selling stocks, you could break the buy or sell order into pieces and manage the risk by placing the purchase with other related instruments in a derivative. Luckily, this formula was perfect for the computer age and allowed the chaps who could afford such technologies to trade bits of equities. This was no big deal as the processors back then were not very sophisticated – a mainframe would have been the equivalent of your Nokia mobile of five years ago – but it did allow some complex analysis to begin. In particular, it allowed the age of leverage to start, and introduced new disciplines in market and credit risk.

This bubbling area of derivatives and risk didn't really take off until the 1990s, when systems had become more and more distributed, powerful and capable. Such systems enabled the chaps to do more hedging and complex investment strategies began. This was further supported by electronic trading, which had also increased in prevalence after the automation of the main markets in New York and London known, over here, as the Big Bang.

Now things were getting a little more efficient, and markets started referring to exotics and "the Greeks". And risk became more destructive as a result with Nick Leeson destroying Barings Bank; Long Term Capital Management (LTCM) almost blew up the financial world; Frank Quattrone was indicted over the internet boom for misrepresenting IPOs; and Henry Blodget got into trouble for mixing securities research with securities trading.

What was really happening is that the mixture of market greed and gaps in regulations allowed many to create more and more complex risk. Risk management was evolving and trying to keep up, as were the lawmakers, but creative and innovative masters of the universe were seeing the opportunity to combine processing power and automated trading with arbitrage and exotic instruments to create ever increasing returns at the expense of those who did not have the ability to make these combinations work.

And yes, there were some big deals like LTCM but the markets coped.

That was until David Li's formula cropped up. David Li's formula is the one that almost killed Wall Street. It is a big deal as it created a number of false assumptions and operations. First, it made traders believe credit risk was managed and covered, when it wasn't. Second, it ignored real world assets to simulated models, and hence separated two key areas that were mutually inclusive and made them mutually exclusive. Third, it didn't incorporate the new forms of market risk we now look towards, namely liquidity risk and systemic risk.

And the real issue that occurred is that the trading systems leveraged the formula to death because, just as this formula was released, electronic trading moved a step forward into algorithmic trading and high frequency trading. This is why the FSA's

Prudential Risk Report 2011 shows that credit went through the roof over the last 40 years.

Similarly, worldwide, OTC derivatives exploded from a market worth $100 trillion in 2000 to $300 trillion in 2005, growing at 30% year on year. It then gathered momentum to grow at 40% percent per annum from 2005 through 2008 reaching a peak of almost $700 trillion when the crisis hit.

This debt and credit explosion was a result of the dangerous concoction of leverage, OTC derivatives, unregulated markets, complex analytics and unlimited processing capacity. This heady mixture had stepped up the financial game into markets that were unmanageable.

From a systems viewpoint, the technology enabled and supported this explosion but was not the cause. The cause is the humans who program the systems. But the systems capabilities are illustrated well by the fact that, in 2000, the New York markets were processing around 5,000 electronic trade movements per second. This has now risen to levels of over ten million per second.

The financial markets have flared up server processing on an unprecedented scale.

For example, RBS Global Banking & Markets are using over 20,000 server blades for core market processing today, compared to a single processor two decades ago.

And,those processors are now operating at near the speed of light. The speed of light travels at around 299,729,458 metres per second, or near 300,000 kilometres per second, so systems are moving trades around at about 270,000 kilometres a second.

Pretty darned fast if you ask me.

So, we have these completely automated systems processing everything in lightning fast speeds globally with all the opportunities for a bit of a byte of a stock or commodity being built into complex arbitrage systems with unlimited scale and processing power.

Sounds like a recipe for a disaster, if you ask me. And it has been. But it's also been a recipe to allow some firms, such as Goldman Sachs, to generate $100 million profit every day that they're open for business. Consistently.

So where does this leave us? In a bit of a bind, I guess. We're not going to get rid of these systems, processors and capabilities, are we? But equally, can we effectively control and regulate them?

I think not. As the general counsel of Salomon Smith Barney is quoted in 'Liar's Poker': "My role is to find the chinks in the regulator's armour", and that attitude prevails. So whilst systems look for chinks, the fragmentation, complexity and geographic spread of systems and regulations allow for arbitrage ... and that makes money.

This is why there is no way to demand and force transparency on the markets. For all the calls of the FSA for real-time liquidity reporting, that reporting is meaningless if the Shanghai or San Paolo operation of the financial firm is leveraged to the hilt.

And the idea of a global response to this is also unlikely. As one speaker said here: "I don't trust any solutions that claim to be global as most global projects fail". Maybe he was involved in the GSTPA or similar ventures.

So the solution: to continue to try to regulate in hindsight and hope that the banks, in foresight, don't create unsustainable or unmanageable risks.

Or just pray!

The credit crisis was NOT a Black Swan event (2010)

One of my holiday books – I'm so geeky dull when it comes to banking – is 'Traders, Guns and Money, Knowns and Unknowns in the Dazzling World of Derivatives', by Satyajit Das. It was recommended to me a while ago, and has been sitting on the bookshelf ever since, like so many books I buy.

This one intrigued me however, as it was written way back in February 2006, 18 months before the August 2007 run on Northern Rock and two-and-a-half years before the September 2008 implosion of Lehman Brothers.

So Nassim Taleb talks about a Black Swan crisis ... this one wasn't. This crisis was thoroughly predictable, as 'Traders, Guns and Money' makes clear.

I dived straight in to the last chapter on Credit Default Swaps (CDS) and Collateralised Debt Obligations (CDO), one of my favourite subjects. There's a good note in there on page 295 about these suckers. Here's a shortened version of that note:

> "CDO logic is perverse. You buy loans and other credit risk from the market, then you cut it and dice it and sell it to investors. It should be impossible to make money. Then why are CDOs so profitable?

> "In the credit trading age, dealers were taking massive 'model risk' to provide investors with higher returns. It was the geeks and their masters who were writing the cheques; they had placed their faith in the credit models; they had started to believe in their lies. Perversely, they were showing massive profits. That's the beauty of mark-to-model. If the model fails, the profit will disappear like a chimera.

> "In 2002 and 2003, benign conditions in the credit market prevailed. Few companies defaulted; people became foolish or brave and lent to companies at ever lower returns; the credit spread on junk bonds reached record lows. Credit standards declined.

> "In 2004, one bank suffered a loss of around $50 million in a single day on its credit dealt books. Nobody really knew why: it was the first tremor."

You get the idea. This book explained all the background to why we would see a subprime explosion and liquidity crisis ... back in February 2006, charting events going back to 2004 and before.

The book cites a court case from 2004 for example, where Barclays Capital were sued by German investment fund, HSH, for 'misrepresentation' after BarCap lost $151 million on one of their CDOs:

> "HSH claims it was mis-sold the products, known as col-lateralised debt obligations (CDOs), and that Barclays then mismanaged its portfolio of CDOs in a way which further damaged the interests of investors. Barclays also stands accused of 'short-selling' the CDOs for its own commercial benefit."

Barclays argued that the losses were just due to the 'unexpected' downturn in the credit markets, and that HSH was a sophisticated investor and aware of the risks. Doesn't this sound like Goldman Sachs today?

"The risk associated with the securities was known to these investors, who were among the most sophisticated mortgage investors in the world" – Goldman Sachs April 16th press release, in response to the SEC's accusations.

It's a standard defence, as was BarCap's response that it would "vigorously defend" the action as they were "comfortable that these investments were not mis-sold". In 2004, Barclays settled the case with HSH a few weeks before it came to trial as they wanted to avoid the headlines.

A similar case was brought against Barclays and Bank of America at this time by the Italian Banca Popolare di Intra. Again, it was settled out of court.

If you're interested in this stuff, there's a really good presenta-tion on CDO litigation from Jones Day, a law firm, at a London conference in March 2008.

14

Here's some of the content.

What triggers litigation?
- Unexpected and large potential losses;
- Tripping of over-collateralization or similar tests;
- Disagreement over appropriate priority of payments;
- Liquidation of portfolio assets;
- Collateral calls;
- Poor documentation where ambiguity = opportunity;
- An unwillingness to compromise or inability to do so due to an encumbered balance sheet.

What are the claims?
America's claims are based upon:
- Sales practices –
  - Misrepresentations and omissions;
  - Collateral contracts/promissory estoppel;
  - Suitability;
- Federal securities fraud claims;
- Mismanagement; Breach of fiduciary duty;
- Breach of contract –
  - Contract interpretation;
  - Third party beneficiary standing;
- Aiding and abetting breach of fiduciary duty/fraud;
- Civil conspiracy;
- Class actions?

UK claims are based upon:
- Deceit;
- Misrepresentation (if contract) based upon being innocent/negligent/fraudulent;
- Breach of contract: contract term/implied term (reasonable skill and care in management of funds);
- Negligent mis-statement (if no contract);
- Breach of a duty of good faith/duty to inform.

*The Extraordinary Madness of Banks and the
Extreme Folly of Governments*

Who brings the claims?

- CDO investors –
  - Senior Note holders vs. Income Note holders;
  - Institutional vs. individual investors;
  - Hedge funds/ fund investors;
  - Liquidators and trustees of insolvent CDOs;
- Swap counterparties;
- Monoline insurers;
- Warehouse agents.

Who gets sued?

- Placement agents\underwriter;
- Portfolio managers;
- Financial advisors;
- Administrative agents;
- CDO directors and officers;
- Rating agencies;
- Mono-line insurers;
- Accountants;
- Other professionals? Law firms?

Interesting, and I'll bet this rumbles on for years to come.

Meanwhile, if all this was rumbling along back in 2004 such that a book could be written about it in February 2006, how come no-one – including yours truly – knew what was really happening until the poop hit the fan?

The credit crisis was NOT a Black Swan event (Part Two) (2010)

Could we have forecast the credit crisis? Yes.

Ten years ago in the US, Sandy Weill put great pressure on Bill Clinton's office to repeal the Glass-Steagall Act with some success. This was because Sandy had a vision for Citigroup, which had grown from a retail bank to an integrated bank and insurer thanks to the merger with Travellers.

Sandy now wanted to create a global universal bank, integrating insurance, securities and retail banking, with Citibank, Travellers and Salamon Smith Barney at the forefront.

Trouble was that his plans were being thwarted by regulations, as Glass-Steagall prohibited any one institution from acting as a combination of investment bank, commercial bank and insurance company. This ruling was made after the 1929 Great Depression and stock market crash.

After years of lobbying, Weill was successful, and the Glass-Steagall Act was repealed and Gramm-Leach-Bliley (GLB) came into force. The GLB Act allowed commercial banks, investment banks, securities firms and insurance companies to consolidate, and therefore created the legal platform for Citigroup to emerge.

At the time, we thought the revolutionary model the Act would enable was bancassurance, where more banks would offer full service in-house insurance. Instead, it allowed the riskier activities of the investment markets to infect the rest of the financial operations.

These risky activities would infect the rest of the financial ops regardless – just look at Long Term Capital Management (LTCM) – as the markets are like a house of cards. However, it did create a significant step towards the crash situation we are dealing with today.

Did no-one object? Sure, a few did and, today, the US senator Byron Dorgan is being accredited as the visionary. Here's an extract of what he had to say back in 1999:

> "I spoke earlier today about this legislation, which is called the Financial Services Modernization Act of 1999, and said then that I am probably part of a very small minority in this Chamber, but I feel very strongly that this is exactly the wrong bill at exactly the wrong time. It misses all the lessons of the

17

past and, in my judgment, it creates definitions and moves in directions that will be counterproductive to our financial future.

"What does this bill do? It would permit common owner-ship of banks, insurance, and securities companies, and, to a significant degree, commercial firms as well. It will permit bank holding companies, affiliates, and bank subsidiaries to engage in a smorgasbord of expanded financial activities, including insurance and securities underwriting, and mer-chant banking all under the same roof.

"This bill will also, in my judgment, raise the likelihood of future massive taxpayer bailouts. It will fuel the con-solidation and mergers in the banking and financial services industry at the expense of customers, farm businesses, family farmers, and others, and in some instances I think it inappro-priately limits the ability of the banking and thrift institution regulators from monitoring activities between such insti-tutions and their insurance or securities affiliates and sub-sidiaries raising significant safety and soundness consumer protection concerns."

And further proof from the *New York Times* at that time:

Congress passes wide-ranging Bill easing bank laws
By Stephen Labaton, November 5, 1999

"WASHINGTON, Nov. 4— Congress approved landmark legislation today that opens the door for a new era on Wall Street in which commercial banks, securities houses and insurers will find it easier and cheaper to enter one another's businesses.

"The measure, considered by many the most important banking legislation in 66 years, was approved in the Senate by a vote of 90 to 8 and in the House tonight by 362 to 57.

18

The bill will now be sent to the president, who is expected to sign it, aides said. It would become one of the most significant achievements this year by the White House and the Republicans leading the 106th Congress.

" 'Today Congress voted to update the rules that have governed financial services since the Great Depression and replace them with a system for the 21st century,' Treasury Secretary Lawrence H. Summers said. 'This historic legislation will better enable American companies to compete in the new economy.' "

"The decision to repeal the Glass-Steagall Act of 1933 provoked dire warnings from a handful of dissenters that the deregulation of Wall Street would someday wreak havoc on the nation's financial system. The original idea behind Glass-Steagall was that separation between bankers and brokers would reduce the potential conflicts of interest that were thought to have contributed to the speculative stock frenzy before the Depression.

"Today's action followed a rich Congressional debate about the history of finance in America in this century, the causes of the banking crisis of the 1930s, the globalization of banking and the future of the nation's economy.

"Administration officials and many Republicans and Democrats said the measure would save consumers billions of dollars and was necessary to keep up with trends in both domestic and international banking. Some institutions, like Citigroup, already have banking, insurance and securities arms but could have been forced to divest their insurance underwriting under existing law. Many foreign banks already enjoy the ability to enter the securities and insurance industries.

" 'The world changes, and we have to change with it,' said Senator Phil Gramm of Texas, who wrote the law that will bear his name along with the two other main Republican sponsors, Representative Jim Leach of Iowa and Representative Thomas J. Bliley Jr. of Virginia. 'We have a new century coming, and we have an opportunity to dominate that century the same way we dominated this century. Glass-Steagall, in the midst of the Great Depression, came at a time when the thinking was that the government was the answer. In this era of economic prosperity, we have decided that freedom is the answer.'

"In the House debate, Mr. Leach said, 'This is a historic day. The landscape for delivery of financial services will now surely shift.'

"But consumer groups and civil rights advocates criticized the legislation for being a sop to the nation's biggest financial institutions. They say that it fails to protect the privacy interests of consumers and community lending standards for the disadvantaged and that it will create more problems than it solves.

"The opponents of the measure gloomily predicted that by unshackling banks and enabling them to move more freely into new kinds of financial activities, the new law could lead to an economic crisis down the road when the marketplace is no longer growing briskly.

" 'I think we will look back in 10 years' time and say we should not have done this but we did because we forgot the lessons of the past, and that that which is true in the 1930s is true in 2010,' said Senator Byron L. Dorgan, Democrat of North Dakota. 'I wasn't around during the 1930s or the debate over Glass-Steagall. But I was here in the early 1980s when it was decided to allow the expansion of savings and loans. We have now decided in the name of modernization to forget the lessons of the past, of safety and of soundness.'

"Senator Paul Wellstone, Democrat of Minnesota, said that Congress had 'seemed determined to unlearn the lessons from our past mistakes.'

" 'Scores of banks failed in the Great Depression as a result of unsound banking practices, and their failure only deepened the crisis,' Mr. Wellstone said. 'Glass-Steagall was intended to protect our financial system by insulating commercial banking from other forms of risk. It was one of several stabilizers designed to keep a similar tragedy from recurring. Now Congress is about to repeal that economic stabilizer without putting any comparable safeguard in its place.'

"Supporters of the legislation rejected those arguments. They responded that historians and economists have concluded that the Glass-Steagall Act was not the correct response to the banking crisis because it was the failure of the Federal Reserve in carrying out monetary policy, not speculation in the stock market, that caused the collapse of 11,000 banks. If anything, the supporters said, the new law will give financial companies the ability to diversify and therefore reduce their risks. The new law, they said, will also give regulators new tools to supervise shaky institutions.

" 'The concerns that we will have a meltdown like 1929 are dramatically overblown,' said Senator Bob Kerrey, Democrat of Nebraska.

"Others said the legislation was essential for the future leadership of the American banking system.

" 'If we don't pass this bill, we could find London or Frankfurt or years down the road Shanghai becoming the financial

The Extraordinary Madness of Banks and the
Extreme Folly of Governments

capital of the world,' said Senator Charles E. Schumer, Democrat of New York. 'There are many reasons for this bill, but first and foremost is to ensure that US financial firms remain competitive.'

(...)

"Many experts predict that, even though the legislation has been trailing market trends that have begun to see the cross-ownership of banks, securities firms and insurers, the new law is certain to lead to a wave of large financial mergers.

"The White House has estimated the legislation could save consumers as much as $18 billion a year as new financial conglomerates gain economies of scale and cut costs.

"Other experts have disputed those estimates as overly optimistic, and said that the bulk of any profits seen from the deregulation of financial services would be returned not to customers but to shareholders."

(...)

What do criminals, bankers and Warren Buffett have in common? (2010)

Some years ago, I delivered a presentation as a keynote with the title 'All Bankers are Criminals'. I actually didn't mean 'all'. The chicken feed, battery farmed, commercial, transactional and retail bankers are pin-stripe suited, humble pie, nice guys.

I was talking about the evil animals of Wall Street and the City. These jungle animals hunt you down, rip out your wallet and tear your money apart, note-by-note. OK, I exaggerate a little, but you get the idea.

The theme of the presentation mainly came from Frank Partnoy's excellent book 'Infectious Greed', which traces the growth of 'weapons of financial destruction': derivatives, as named by Warren Buffett in his 2002 shareholder letter.

It is quite clear from this book that unchecked investment markets will run free of scruples and morals. This is what happened with Frank Quattrone of Credit Suisse and the dotcom boom and bust, along with many other examples through history.

It is not necessarily as true when we talk about arbitrage strategies and the John Meriwethers of this world. However, these people are far more dangerous because they create financial markets systemic risk that can bring down companies and countries.

In case you are wondering who John Meriwether is, he was one of the first arbitrage players and built Salomon Brothers into the big swinging dick master of the universe world so brilliantly depicted in Michael Lewis's book 'Liar's Poker'.

With his colleagues, the use of arbitrage instruments led to the downfall of Salomon Brothers – they were subsequently merged into Citigroup – and Meriwether went on to create Long Term Capital Management (LTCM).

In 1998 LTCM lost $4.6 billion in less than four months and became the leading case study for how systemic risk created by derivatives products, combined with massive leverage and arbitrage risk-models, creates a financial deck of cards. A deck that can rise and fall in the blink of an eye, with the latter potentially ruining companies, markets, countries and governments, as happened in the most recent crisis.

Anyways, not to be dissuaded from his cause, Meriwether went on to found JWM Partners, another highly leveraged 'relative value arbitrage' firm. Yet again, he built leverage through this hedge fund from its opening with $250 million under management in 1999 to a massive $3 billion firm by 2007. Of course, it was all just on paper as the latest crisis battered the fund, losing almost half of its value between September 2007 and February 2009. The deck of cards strikes again.

It closed in late 2009 and guess what? Meriwether's about to launch yet another hedge fund, based upon just the same concepts.

To me, this is the criminality of the financial system in action. Firms that build highly leveraged derivatives instruments for short-term arbitrage, with unproven skills and massive risk.

Not that I'm calling Meriwether a criminal, as it's all perfectly legitimate under SEC and FSA rules. Or it was. It may be that the Goldman Sachs furore will change all this.

You see, Goldman Sachs, like Meriwether, is very good at taking leverage and risk and managing the markets to gain short-term profit. Like Meriwether, Goldman Sachs succeeded in using these tools and instruments to generate massive profits. They achieved a record 131 trading days last year, in which the bank made at least $100 million net trading revenue each day.

Unlike Meriwether, Goldman Sachs managed to offload and hedge their risks back to others, such as AIG and IKB, such that when the markets collapsed, their clients, suppliers and partners got burnt, but not them.

Nothing wrong with that, as it's all perfectly legitimate under SEC and FSA rules. Unless the SEC and FSA find Goldman Sachs guilty of fraud. But how can they be guilty of a crime that was not a crime at the time it was committed? There's the rub.

I'm sure the SEC will aim to build a bulletproof case, and their cause is a worthy one: clean up the financial system.

Is it worthy to do this so publicly? Not sure. Is it worthy to name the defendant up front, when the burden of proof has yet to be proven? Not sure.

The Goldman Sachs case is actually more like watching a rape trial in action, where the defendant is a shifty-looking guy who probably seems guilty whether guilty or not. The guilt sits there, and that's what will happen with Goldman Sachs.

Whether guilty or not – and they've hired the best team possible to defend themselves, including 'Master of Disaster' Mark Fabiani – we will always associate Goldman Sachs with something smelly for the foreseeable years to come.

The only thing that really gets me is Warren Buffett. The Sage of Omaha has made his billions through prudent focus upon 'value investing'. That means investing in strong and robust businesses like Coca-Cola, American Express, Gillette and the *Washington Post*.

So when he referred to derivatives as 'weapons of financial destruction' in his shareholder letter of 2002, I respected the man and his integrity of thought. Now, having found Goldman Sachs under attack, he has stepped up to their defence, and I wondered why.

Warren Buffett is an intriguing character, as we all know. The friend of kings and kingmakers, he walks a path separate to most. He knows the dangers of arbitrage, derivatives and leverage, because he had to step into Salomon Brothers in 1991 to clean up Meriwether and his colleagues' mess.

(...)

Switch to 2010. Warren Buffett invested heavily in Goldman Sachs in September 2008 – when Lehman Brothers, Merrill Lynch and Morgan Stanley were all imploding – buying $5 billion of preferred stock at a 10 percent dividend. These investments earn him $950 a minute, or $500 million a year today. No wonder he claims to be in love with that investment.

Trouble is that the alleged fraud at Goldman Sachs has really hit their share price.

Thinking back to the observation on Salomon that if *the firm* is 'credit dependent', as Salomon was to an extreme, it cannot tolerate a negative change in perceptions, Buffett must be seriously worried about Goldman Sachs losing its creditworthiness, especially as it depends on good credit.

Oh yes, and having called derivatives 'weapons of financial destruction', guess what? Berkshire Hathaway, Warren Buffett's investment firm, has a massive portfolio of derivatives investments. From the *Wall Street Journal* last week:

> "Democrats took a step toward their goal of overhauling financial regulation, reaching a tentative deal to set restrictions on trading in exotic financial instruments known as derivatives. Among the considerations still in the balance: A big provision being sought by Warren Buffett in recent weeks ... the provision, sought by Berkshire and pushed by Nebraska Senator Ben Nelson in the Senate Agriculture Committee, would largely exempt existing derivatives contracts from the proposed rules. Previously, the legislation could have allowed regulators to require that companies such as Nebraska-based Berkshire put aside large sums to cover potential losses. The change thus would aid Berkshire, which has a $63 billion derivatives portfolio, according to Barclays Capital."

Hmmm ... maybe that greed is infectious, although Morningstar analyst Bill Bergman supports Mr. Buffett's exemption by stating that: "Claiming Berkshire poses a risk to the financial system is a difficult case to make."

Either way, the US movement towards an approval of a Financial Reform Bill to handle the issues of banks that are 'too big to fail' takes it one step nearer to the American system taking a lead role towards a new financial architecture.

Derivatives are next ... and Warren Buffett, like Lloyd Blankfein at Goldman Sachs and all of those current and former bankers and brokers who dealt in toxic derivatives across the world, must be worried.

Who can be trusted after the financial crisis? (2009)

Just found a great paper by the Centre for European Policy Studies (CEPS) titled 'Who can be trusted after the financial crisis?' Using extensive research across the EU, the EC, the ECB and more, they draw four main conclusions.

"First, our analysis of the impact of the financial crisis on confidence in the European institutions shows a severe decrease in citizens' trust in the immediate aftermath of the financial crisis with a slight recovery nine month later. In particular citizens' net trust in the ECB hit an historical low point in the aftermath of the financial crisis with a majority of people distrusting the ECB.

"Second, the trend in confidence in European institutions is diametrically opposed to citizens' confidence in the national government and parliament. When citizens' confidence in the European institutions decreased in the immediate aftermath of the crisis, confidence in the national government actually increased. When the confidence in European institutions recovered nine months later, confidence in the national government decreased. However, not all data support this conclusion. Data from the Edelman Trust Barometer suggest a continuous increase in the confidence in the government.

"Third, our analysis of confidence in business and citizens' confidence in banks and stock markets produces ambiguous results. Whereas citizens' confidence in stock markets and business confidence has recovered in most countries, confidence in banks has deteriorated nine month after the crisis.

"Fourth, confidence levels in free market economies seem to have dropped in a majority of countries nine month after the crisis. Only in the German case could one actually detect an

The Extraordinary Madness of Banks and the Extreme Folly of Governments

increase in confidence in the free market economy. However, separate data sources show that levels of net confidence in the free market economy in the US remain significantly higher than in the two European economies Germany and France.

"Given that in particular in France and Germany a decrease in net confidence is associated with an increase in citizens' demands for stronger state support and that German and French citizens have the highest level of anti-capitalist sentiments, French and German governments will have to invest more effort in trust enhancing policies.

"Nevertheless, one has to highlight that the financial crisis also had a deep impact on the US economy as citizens' demand for stronger state regulation has risen immensely and has almost reached European levels."

Queen to chair debate about capitalism killing the planet? (2009)

On 22nd July, Fellows of the British Academy Professors Tim Besley, FBA, and Peter Hennessy, FBA, sent a letter to Her Majesty the Queen (heavily edited version follows):

"Madam

When Your Majesty visited the London School of Economics last November, you quite rightly asked: why had nobody noticed that the credit crunch was on its way? The British Academy convened a forum on 17 June 2009 to debate your question.

Many people did foresee the crisis. However, the exact form that it would take and the timing of its onset and ferocity were foreseen by nobody.

For example, the Bank of International Settlements expressed repeated concerns that risks did not seem to be properly reflected in financial markets. Our own Bank of England issued many warnings about this in their biannual Financial Stability Reports.

Risk management was considered an important part of financial markets. One of our major banks, now mainly in public ownership, reputedly had 4,000 risk managers. But the difficulty was seeing the risk to the system as a whole rather than to any specific financial instrument or loan. Risk calculations were most often confined to slices of financial activity, using some of the best mathematical minds in our country and abroad. But they frequently lost sight of the bigger picture.

There were many who warned of the dangers of this. But against those who warned, most were convinced that banks knew what they were doing.

They believed that the financial wizards had found new and clever ways of managing risks. Indeed, some claimed to have so dispersed them through an array of novel financial instruments that they had virtually removed them. It is difficult to recall a greater example of wishful thinking combined with hubris.

And politicians of all types were charmed by the market. People trusted the banks whose boards and senior executives were packed with globally recruited talent and their non-executive directors included those with proven track records in public life. Nobody wanted to believe that their judgement could be faulty or that they were unable competently to scrutinise the risks in the organisations that they managed. A generation of bankers and financiers deceived themselves

*The Extraordinary Madness of Banks and the
Extreme Folly of Governments*

and those who thought that they were the pace-making engineers of advanced economies.

All this exposed the difficulties of slowing the progression of such developments in the presence of a general 'feel-good' factor.

 Among the authorities charged with managing these risks, there were difficulties too. Some say that their job should have been 'to take away the punch bowl when the party was in full swing'. But that assumes that they had the instruments needed to do this. General pressure was for more lax regulation – a light touch. The City of London (and the Financial Services Authority) was praised as a paragon of global financial regulation for this reason.

There was a broad consensus that it was better to deal with the aftermath of bubbles in stock markets and housing markets than to try to head them off in advance.

Inflation remained low and created no warning sign of an economy that was overheating.

 So where was the problem?

 Everyone seemed to be doing their own job properly on its own merit. And according to standard measures of success, they were often doing it well. The failure was to see how collectively this added up to a series of interconnected imbalances over which no single authority had jurisdiction. This, combined with the psychology of herding and the mantra of financial and policy gurus, lead to a dangerous recipe. Individual risks may rightly have been viewed as small, but the risk to the system as a whole was vast.

 So in summary, Your Majesty, the failure to foresee the timing, extent and severity of the crisis and to head it off, while it had many causes, was principally a failure of the collective imagination of many bright people, both in this country and internationally, to understand the risks to the system as a whole."

Very good.

On 14th August 2009, a group of senior figures including Professor Herman Daly of Maryland University, Professor Lord Anthony Giddens and Professor Peter Victor of York University, Canada, sent this letter (heavily edited) to the Queen:

"Your Majesty,

We, the undersigned, noted with interest the letter to Your Majesty of 22nd July 2009 from the British Academy in which they respond to your question about how the current economic meltdown was missed. They talked of a "failure of the collective imagination of many bright people" and a "psychology of denial". The Academy wrote "It is difficult to recall a greater example of wishful thinking combined with hubris."

We are writing to you because we are concerned that the British Academy's letter focuses on one particular aspect of current insecurity, namely financial, failing to address the wider context of more serious macro issues facing mankind. We are also writing to the Academy to invite them to debate these issues with us.

We live in tumultuous times. Many developed world citizens are losing their livelihoods. The effects on the world's poorest will, as ever, be dreadful. However, we are surprised that the Academy has not addressed anything outside the narrow remit their letter covered. Far greater insecurities threaten the world's poorest due to our effects on the natural world.

The letter ignores the physical constraints which are central to this bubble and indeed most bubbles. It speaks of "the bigger picture" and of "individual risks being small" and "the system as a whole being vast", yet, for us has a limited horizon.

Our premise is that our current economic malaise is symptomatic of a far more serious systemic failure to acknowledge what Archbishop Rowan Williams has identified in saying "It has been said that 'the economy is a wholly-owned subsidiary of the environment'. The earth itself is what ultimately controls economic activity because it is the source of the materials upon which economic activity works".

Energy is the lifeblood of any economy. Our exponential debt-based money system is in turn based on exponentially increasing energy supplies. It is therefore clear that the supply of that energy deserves our very highest attention. That this attention doesn't appear in the Academy's analysis is deeply worrying.

The letter refers to the "overheating economy" but gives no mention of the effect and cause of the overheating of planet Earth.

The Academy's letter mentions unprecedented global economic growth – yet it fails to mention the rapidly escalating environmental destruction caused by this insatiable growth. It also mentions the poor of the developing world who have been brought out of poverty to 'prosperity'; but not the far greater numbers condemned to an increasingly inequitable world and the ravages of peak-food and climate change.

The letter talks of a "general feel-good factor", but doesn't address the fact that, in the developed world, general wellbeing long ago ceased to be linked with GDP growth.

We envisage a society whose primary goal should be the wellbeing of society itself and of the planetary resources and environment that sustains us all, with economic objectives shaped to support that central goal rather than the other way around."

Our current form of corporate-consumer-capitalism has been shown to be what many of us knew it was: a fundamentally flawed system which badly needs updating.

It would appear from the British Academy's letter that they are not aware of the rapidly growing and vibrant debate around these issues. We agree with them about the need for "authorities with the power to act" and for appropriate levels of regulation fit for the task in hand. Their prescription is to consider how they "might develop a new, shared horizon-scanning capability". We will invite the Academy to join with us in a public dialogue about these issues and ask them to consider how this 'new capability' can make its primary horizon the issues we raise in this letter. We will of course report findings of such debate to Your Majesty."

I wonder if the Queen could be the chair in a nice debate entitled 'This House believes that capitalism is killing the planet'?

BBC's Robert Peston presents ... (2009)

Robert Peston, the BBC's lead reporter on the banks throughout this crisis and author of 'Who Runs Britain?' presented a discussion I attended the other night.

Robert's presentation was titled 'The new capitalism: the cost of men behaving badly' and, just to be clear, he presented under Chatham House rules so the summary below is purely my spin on what he said, and not his words.

First, an estimate of the losses to date. $4 trillion. Actually, no, it was $9 trillion. That's $9,000,000,000,000.

The Extraordinary Madness of Banks and the Extreme Folly of Governments

If a dollar was equivalent to one second, it would take about 11.57 days to get through a million dollars, 31.7 years to get through a billion and back to the birth of mankind 32,000 years ago to get to a trillion dollars. That's $1 trillion.

$9 trillion. $9 trillion of losses. $4 trillion came from the banking industry. $4 trillion of bailouts, cash injections, support and relief. Then a further $5 trillion of corporate losses in lost output through lack of access to liquidity, loans, working capital and trade finance.

$9 trillion. About 300,000 years of spending a dollar a second. That's 25% of the world's global output.

A quarter of the world's output lost due to this silly crisis created by what? Bad maths.

This is best illustrated by the example of Goldman Sachs' black box event back in August 2007. This is where David Viniar, Goldman Sachs' CFO, said: "We are seeing things that were 25-standard deviation events, several days in a row. There have been some issues in some of the other quantitative spaces, but nothing like what we saw last week."

A '25-standard deviation event' only happens once every 100,000 years or more according to the models built into the systems, but then they occurred several days in a row and the Goldman Sachs fund lost $1.5 billion.

In other words, banks were organised and managed using bad science. Now, was that down to too little regulation – 'light touch' – or just bad regulation? To be truthful, it is an indictment of regulation that didn't work combined with a failure of Alan Greenspan's science.

You see, Greenspan prayed to the lords of securitisation and light touch regulation. He believed markets regulated themselves through competitive forces and securitisation worked because it distributes risks widely across the markets. But there were two errors in Greenspan's thinking that went wrong.

The first was the belief that banks only lent money after checking that a borrower had the ability to pay it back; and the other was the belief that banks would lay off risks to others and spread the risks widely across the markets.

The banks did not do this. In fact, they retained risks because, once this was repackaged and given a AAA rating, it was easier to keep on the banks' books as assets rather than spreading them around outside the markets.

And in all cases, the regulators missed this trick because they were looking for crooks rather than idiots. This was not criminal activity, just incompetence, and the FSA and SEC just thought management of these firms were regulating their staff misbehaviours rather than looking for such malfeasance. This is why we expect too much from regulation as, to be honest, there was more regulation than you could shake a stick at before this crisis, and much of it was on a statutory footing.

So this was a failure of regulators, regulation, management and markets ... but the overall failure was not caused by these factors, but more by a failure of theory.

This is because conventional analysis saw the housing and market bubble as harmless, and the theory was that the housing market wouldn't need to be propped up by the Bank of England. But that theory was wrong due to the fact that there was far too much lending at far too cheap a price, and the theory that liquidity would remain stable and available was wrong.

The result is that we borrowed more than 100% of GDP and personal sector borrowing today is running at around 170% of GDP. That's ridiculous. It has increased by around 70% since 2000, and it was unhealthy back in 2000 as a result of eight years of unparalleled growth in the economy.

So here is the horrible paradox: compliance meant that any banker would tell you that regulation was severe and intrusive. The result is that we bred a culture of compliance where, if the boxes were ticked and all ok, then the deal was ok. This meant that no-one asked whether the deal was sensible or ethical, in a more fundamental sense.

It was this culture of box ticking that resulted in the biggest regulatory failure any of us will ever witness. But it was more than this, because the box ticking issue lay with the false comfort provided by experts.

The credit rating agencies priesthood meant that even the Bank of England paid homage to these priests. They gave the best AAA ratings, which were meant to be for the nicest investments, to the stinkiest investments. The AAA rating was given to stinky products because of lousy data and a confusion between solvency and liquidity.

The primary thing they got wrong was using data for defaults and repayment difficulties from the 1990s. This data was created when the market was only worth a few billion dollars and it said the market default rate for mortgage repayments would be the same for a massive market, doubling every year, as it was for this tiny market. In other words, the data was extrapolated from a very small sample to a much bigger one.

In retrospect, it was a classic error. Another part of the error was the assumption was that an investment could be sold at any time to create solvency. This belief was that money tied up in assets could be turned into cash fast ... but you cannot do that when liquidity disappears, which is why the losses and rescues occurred because banks thought solvent were not. The belief they were solvent was based upon a belief in their asset liquidity, which just wasn't there.

This is due to the alphabet soup of CDOs, CLOs, SIVs, ABS, RMBS, CMBS, and CDS. These instruments all packaged up risk and allowed banks to borrow short and lend long. There's the rub, because if everyone wants their money back, you don't have it, with all of these Structured Investment Vehicles exacerbating it all.

The capital question is also of huge importance to all of us, even though almost no-one took any interest. This is because most people don't understand how banks work.

Under international rules, banks can lend a part of their capital but must keep some back in case it was to the wrong people. The issue with this is that no single issue in bank regulation is more important than this one, and yet no-one knows the answer as to what is the right level of capital a bank must retain.

We've had Basel and Basel II, and still there was a shortage of capital. That shortage is the reason for this crisis. Have you ever heard a politician discuss bank capital before this crisis?

This failure to debate the most basic question in our system has been the core of this crisis. Those basic questions are how much capital should banks hold, and how much capital in total do banks need to retain to cover their total lending?

This is why liquidity was ignored as no-one believed liquidity could just dry up.

And what happens if everyone asks for their money back all at the same time? Especially if those making the request are your counterparties, those who have the major exposures to each other?

That's what the issue was, and this is what caused the biggest run since 1913 on the financial system. It was because liquidity dried up, all the counterparty banks asked for their money back, and many banks just did not have the capital or access to assets for solvency to cover their exposures.

There were other factors but, generally, the false comfort of statistics and maths was a systematic distribution of common sense. This is why people didn't ask the stupid questions such as: if we are lending two to three times the buffers of capital we used to, why? Where's the protection in that?

RBS was leveraged by a factor of 40, and its board thought there was no subprime exposure because they had the illusion of insurance. But their exposure was to insurance, not subprime lenders, which is why they thought this. And the insurers didn't have the resources to make good on subprime loans if the worst happened, so they were taking false comfort too.

The lessons of this crisis are therefore:

♦ Don't be in awe of experts;
♦ Challenge the science; and
♦ Common sense normally trumps statistics.

MSNBC rip into Citi and Vikram Pandit (2009)

The piece below from MSNBC is building inflammation on top of inflammation, after seeing the anger over AIG stirred into real anger with this diatribe. I predict a riot. Here's a transcript.

"Wall Street treated the bailout bill like a national blackmail scheme

March 19: In a Special Comment, Countdown's Keith Olbermann expresses outrage at Wall Street over their continuing misuse of federal bailout money. Olbermann calls for the firing of bank executives and more stringent bank regulation.

Finally tonight, as promised, a Special Comment on the latest atrocity from the banks. The vast, engorged, gluttonous multinational corporations. Whose sneezes can be fatal to our jobs. Whose mistakes can turn us into the homeless. Whose accounting errors can be so panoramic that they can make our economy tremble and force us to hand them billions after billions in a blackmail scheme that has come to be known as "bailout."

Five weeks ago Vikram Pandit, the chief executive officer of Citigroup, went back to Congress, tail seemingly between his legs, and, with entreaty dripping from his voice, announced "I get the new reality and I'll make sure Citi gets it as well."

In point of fact, as Bloomberg News reports today, what Mr. Pandit "got" was a new $10 million executive suite for himself and his key associates.

This is the same Mr. Pandit who said he would show his leadership by accepting compensation of $1 a year. In fact, he then "accepted" a total compensation package for 2008 of $38 million.

Enough!

Mr. Pandit, you're probably just a good actor and a damned liar and a con man. But I'll give you the benefit of the doubt and assume instead, that you just can't tell the difference between $1 and 38 million of them. That would certainly explain the maelstrom into which you, and your colleagues at Citi and your counterparts elsewhere, have gotten us, including the vast majority of us who are innocent bystanders.

Your bank says your new $10 million office is part of a global strategy of space reduction that will ultimately save billions. It seems entirely appropriate to remind everyone, sir, that this promise could be fulfilled by Citi saving $2 a year for a billion years.

God knows you guys have pulled off every other accounting trick every dreamt up by immoral man. You, sir, and the other corporate pirates like you – those who are saved from your obsessive spending and greed and self-aggrandizement by the taxpayer – who then pretend to atone – who then publicly promise good behaviour – and who then revert immediately to the rapaciousness that is your only skill.

You, sir, all of you, need to be fired.

Enough!

And Mr. Pandit's corporation should be cut up into little pieces. And when he and the other ultra-millionaires wonder what hit them, we should make sure they are easily reminded.

*The Extraordinary Madness of Banks and the
Extreme Folly of Governments*

Our representatives should entitle the legislation that ends their moral Ponzi schemes, "The Punish Vikram Pandit Act of 2009."

The far right in this country, without the slightest provocation, screams "socialism," and the sheep who follow it, who do not know what the word means and do not know it is only being used because "communism" now rings laughably hollow. In this cry of fire in a crowded unemployment line, there is outrage.

But there is also licence. They think this is socialism? There is a million miles of reform to go before we hit socialism, but if they're going to call us names whether they apply or not, let's give them real reform.

Break up the banks. Regulate the financial industries, to within an inch of their existences. Roll back corporate legal protections. Make liable the officers of corporations, for their debts, and for their deeds. Resurrect the rallying cry of a hundred years past: bust the trusts!

AIG gives "failure bonuses" to the cretins whose dalliances in derivatives brought the company and part of the nation to her knees? Spin off that division whose traders are owed the 165 million in bonuses, under-fund it, and cause it to go bankrupt.

Enough!

Let those with bonuses owed, stand in line before a bankruptcy referee, and wind up – just as you and I would – with half a cent on the dollar. Northern Trust fires 450 employees in December. Then takes a billion six in bailout money. Sponsors a golf tournament. Flies hundreds of clients to Southern California for private Oscar parties, including the renting of an airplane hangar and the hiring of the group 'Earth, Wind & Fire?'

Enough!

Fire the executives. And fire up the Justice Department to figure out just how much fraud was involved in asking for a billion-six in bailout money when Northern Trust said nothing as the checks were written, even though it knew in advance that millions could be saved by simply cutting the fluff and the trumpery.

Thirteen more companies that took bailouts, signed the mandatory documents that said they owed no back taxes lied turned out, per Congressman John Lewis of Ways and Means today lied – they owe, just among those 13 firms, 220 million in back taxes?

Enough!

Have the IRS take these companies, immediately, to the tax courts to which the rest of us are liable. And strip those ancient, outdated laws of corporation, so that the officers of the corporation are personally liable for their companies' debts, just as you or I would be. And if the monopolies of radio or television rear up to support the corporate structure, to say a contract is a contract, even though that isn't true for a union these days, only for an AIG trader. Take the invisible, unused Sword of Damocles they still fatuously insist hangs over their heads, and make it real.

Enough!

Make sure both sides are heard. Re-regulate the radio and television industries to limit station ownership and demand diversity of management and product. Reinstate the old rules that denied one man all the voices in a public square. End all waivers of multiple ownership of television stations and networks and newspapers in the same market.

And, yes, if a voice of the privileged classes unfairly uses his cable platform to call our neighbours who are the victims of this, "losers", to insist he alone speaks for the real people.

Or if another, indicts without equal time for defence a particular elected official, and then offers himself as a candidate for that very official's seat, in violation of all canons of good or even fair broadcasting then tell the cable industry that the free ride is over and it is time that it too be regulated by the FCC.

Enough!

*The Extraordinary Madness of Banks and the
Extreme Folly of Governments*

To all of you in the corporate boardrooms. Stop viewing the public's reaction to this naked, unhindered robbery of the public coffers, and your audacious, immeasurable sense of proprietorship and entitlement, stop viewing our anger as some kind of brief impediment, some traffic delay that keeps you from your God-given corporate ballpark sponsorships, and perpetually remodelled offices, and the divine right of $38 million "compensation packages."

You, gentlemen and ladies, and not the good and long-suffering average people of this country, you are fomenting rage in this nation. You are the losers in this equation, and the people are the generous ones; they have not assembled in the streets with pitch-forks and flaming torches. You are the ones perceived – understood in a visceral and even transcendent way – as the committers of what is becoming class economic rape.

And heed this one word before these people grow weary of forgiving you, and instead decide to bring the "good life" – which you have built on their backs – crashing down on top of your heads. When the next boardroom needs remodelling, or the next bonus paid, or the next jet purchased, remember that one word:

Enough!"

Alan Greenspan caused this crisis (2009)

Back in November 2007, when Alan Greenspan was running around promoting his book, 'The Age of Turbulence', his kudos was high and standing was great. It was just a year after leaving office and subprime had hit, but folks thought it was just a $300 billion hole ... a mere drop in the ocean.

I heard him speak on the public stage back then, and he made many points all of which came back to "It's not my fault".

Now the crisis is a lot bigger with trillions of dollars involved, and many blame Alan Greenspan for it. For example:

- ◆ 1987, Alan Greenspan assumed office and total outstanding US home mortgages was $1.82 trillion;
- ◆ 1999, total outstanding mortgages in the US was $4.45 trillion;
- ◆ 2004, US home mortgages rose to $7.56 trillion; and in 2005, Greenspan's final full year as Fed chairman, home mortgage debt outstanding increased to $9.1 trillion.

In particular, Alan Greenspan was a fan of the free market system and loose self-regulation, as well as a staunch defender of the use of leverage and derivatives to fuel commerce. He now recognises that there was a flaw in that approach, although some would say he could concede such a point when he has made millions out of the free market system personally.

For example, after leaving office, three firms – Deutsche Bank, Hedge Fund Paulson & Co and bond investment company Pacific Investment Management (PIMCO) – hired Alan Greenspan as an adviser on economic issues and monetary policy. Paulson & Co is known for its record $3.7 billion profit making out of the credit crisis, some of which must have flown the Greenspan way.

With Alan Greenspan's bubble burst, everyone now lays the blame at his feet. This is clearly demonstrated by the media and online rants and raves, with the latest to prompt such outcry coming from two UK newspapers that ran a poll this week to find out who we all think is to blame for this crisis. Alan Greenspan comes out #1 in both. Equally, in a US poll by the *Institutional Investor*, those who should know, 53% blame Greenspan, 28% George W. Bush and, interestingly, 16% Bill Clinton.

What such polls serve to achieve I have no idea, but it does show that Mr. Greenspan might be advised to avoid walking down the street on his own at night for a while.

Chapter 2 Governments in action

Introduction

Following the implosion of the global financial markets, governments rallied together rapidly to try to work out what happened, why, and what to do about it. It was quite sad to watch, really, as many of the governmental players were the same people who created the conditions for the crisis. For example, UK Prime Minister Gordon Brown claimed to be decisive after the failure of Northern Rock, the sudden merger of Lloyds and HBOS and the bailing-out of RBS. However, it was his own actions as Chancellor that allowed the irrational mortgage lending practices of these banks to take place. Similarly in the USA, Alan Greenspan, who ran the Federal Reserve Bank policymaking that led to the sub-prime markets, denied any responsibility for months after the crisis hit, only to eventually realise that it was his total belief in free market practices that had failed. Therefore, when we wonder about the causes of this crisis, much lies firmly at the feet of politicians and policymakers, as they are in charge of the controls that keep markets in check or allow them to fly free and unfettered.

Jim O'Neill on the BRICs - the next decade (2011)

Just tweeted to our friends in the #OccupyLSE group – that's Occupy the London Stock Exchange (LSE) for those who are not aware of the protest outside the LSE at St Paul's – that I attended a meeting at the London Stock Exchange this morning.

Yes, I occupied the LSE! Well, just for an hour in order to hear the thoughts of one Jim O'Neill, Chairman of Goldman Sachs Asset Management.

Jim is the man who coined the term BRICs for the growth countries of Brazil, Russia, India and China ten years ago (his paper was published in November 2001). Since then everyone has taken the success story of China as read, although it has also been

46

noted that the Brazil, Russia and India growth story also came true.

Now, 10 years later, Jim was asked the question by the LSE: "Do BRIC countries still need the West for growth or is the reverse now true?" and this was the theme of his presentation. Here's my spin on his talk (this is not a direct transcription therefore).

The question "Do BRIC countries still need the West for growth or is the reverse now true?", couldn't be more apt after the G20 meeting in Cannes last week. In fact, I would claim that this is **the** most important question facing global economies and leaders today. And my answer is yes, the reverse is true.

The West has been the most challenged since 2008 as their deleveraging crisis has been with them ever since, and the BRICs are an ever-increasing part of the solution.

That being said, the BRICs are living in the same planet as the rest of us and cannot let the West completely implode. For example, as we watch the troubling worlds of Greece and increasingly Italy, the BRICs are seeing more and more impact.

This is especially key for London, in its role in global finance, and is illustrated by the interesting events taking place a few yards away outside St Paul's Cathedral (where the occupy LSE movement is demonstrating), which means it is very important that all of us involved in business and finance get a bit more objective about the issues being discussed in public forum these days.

Over the last decade the nominal increase in GDP amongst the BRICs has been greater than any other group of countries, apart from the G7. This is difficult for people of my generation to see or accept, because it is new, although younger people get it far more easily. Maybe this is because older people find it hard to adapt or change.

During the last decade, the GDP of G7 increased by $11 trillion. Meanwhile, the Growth8 as I call them – the BRICs plus Indonesia, Vietnam, Mexico and Turkey – increased by a similar amount.

These countries are therefore so economically important that it's rather sad and stupid that people still call these countries 'emerging markets' when they have now emerged, and are contributing so much to growth and global markets. We should call them something else, which is why I choose to call them the Growth8, as opposed to other countries which are emerging markets.

BRICs represent 80% of the Growth8's $11 trillion growth in the last decade. The 'C' in particular – China – has seen its GDP increase faster than the USA in the last decade. Another example is Brazil, which has seen GDP increase faster than Germany, Japan and the UK.

From 2010 to 2019, the Growth8 will again rise faster, with China still leading the way. BRICs will see GDP growth of over $12 trillion of the $16 trillion rise in the Growth8, with China contributing around $8 trillion, or half of that GDP growth. This assumes an 8% average growth rate in their economy, so it assumes China's growth will slow down.

However, if you look at the figures, the USA will only grow about $3 trillion in GDP by comparison, and Euroland by under $2 trillion.

In these figures, you would need a magnifying glass to see where Greece would sit in the global economy. It's not big enough to matter. For example, China will grow by the equivalent of three Greeces this year – it creates a new Greece GDP size every four months. Unfortunately, that is not the case with Italy.

Looking to the future, the global share of GDP in 2020 will be 41% for the G7; and 35% for the Growth8. Of these, 27% of global GDP will be with the BRICs; 19% with the USA; 17% for China; and 16% for the whole of Euroland!

So during the next decade, the BRICs will be bigger than the USA. This is important change, and the G20 and IMF are already changing their thinking about the BRICs.

For example, the IMF said at last week's G20 meeting that it is going to review its Special Drawing Rights (SDR) basket of currencies before 2015, when it was next scheduled for review.

This implies that the Remnimbi (RMB) will be brought into the SDR basket before 2015 because China has moved far closer to full convertibility of their currency sooner than expected, which is incredibly important for everyone in finance, whether you invest in China or not.

This means that debt or equity issued in Chinese RMB becomes normal, which is infinitely more important than what's going on in terms of Greek and European politics.

For example, when we berate others about their fiscal affairs we have to be careful, as when you look at the budget deficits and government debt, it is clear that this not a sovereign debt crisis.

The gross government debt as a percentage of GDP in the UK (85%), USA (100%) and Japan (233%) are far worse than in the Eurozone, but their governments still have highly rated sovereign debt.

So the Eurozone issue is more a question of revealing the issue of the weakness of the European Economic & Monetary Union (EMU), rather than a question of sovereign debt.

And if you look at debt in the Growth8, the gross government debt as a percentage of GDP is under 25% for many. This is why these economies are so key to the future and is illustrated by retail sales.

Retail sales since 2007 have dipped significantly in advanced economies but, in growth and emerging markets, are going up rapidly.

This is why German exports in the last four years have seen the biggest rise in sales to China, India and Russia. By 2012, Germany will be exporting more to China than to its neighbour France, which is a real shock.

This demonstrates why the BRICs are now independent of the West and the West needs them far more than they need us.

But the BRICs are not some homogenous area or singular market. Two are democracies and two are not, and their wealth is very different. Brazil and Russia average around $15,000 a head, China $5,000, whilst India is under $2,000; so they are not similar in terms of wealth or politics. Equally, they differ in content, with two commodity producers and two importers, so they are not a region together.

However, the fact that they now meet as a group annually is a symbolic move to Western leaders for change in economic governance, and to have these guys at the centre of it.

For example, the G20 is way too big and ugly, so we need a new G7 or G8, of which the BRICs and China will form a key part. For the UK and Canada that's tough as, in terms of their size of GDP, it makes you wonder what they're doing there.

The real topic now is what's happening to Chinese inflation. It should get under 4% next year, which will be massively important as it will stop China's tightening of monetary policy and will help the global economy as a result.

We should also note that 2020-2029 might be India's decade. China's demographics will create a turndown and growing anywhere near 10% per annum will be tough a decade from now. India has great demographics however, with its working population increasing by the size of the total USA population in a decade.

Finally, political instabilities are a factor in this outlook.

We have a Goldman Sachs Growth Environment Score (GES) that looks at 13 variables related to the sustainability of growth and productivity, and India scores the lowest of the BRICs on this score.

So when people ask me if I was mistaken about Russia being in this list, I respond by saying I'd take the 'I' out of BRICs before the 'R'.

India is challenged in terms of sustainable growth due to government finances and the lack of a credible framework for economic policy. They also have many other issues of corruption and indecisiveness, which means that they can conceptually be a leader by 2020 or after only if they address these challenges first.

Andrew Tyrie: a man with a mission (2010)

Our last meeting of the year at the Financial Services Club featured Andrew Tyrie, Head of the Treasury Select Committee. In a packed room, Andrew talked about the government's challenges and his own varied agenda.

For example, just in the last few days he had witnessed:

◆ European Commissioner for the Internal Markets Michel Barnier get himself into a tangle;

◆ The FSA capitulate to pressure to publish their 'secret' report on the failure of the Royal Bank of Scotland;

◆ A new deal with the Irish government over their bank structures in order to clear a £3.25 billion loan from the UK; and

◆ The founder of Metro Bank, Vernon Hill, telling him that the state of the UK retail banking sector is so uncompetitive that he is going to mop up.

Just an average few days for a Treasury Select Committee Chairman, or maybe not.

As Andrew made clear, he has little time for wishy-washy mishmash. By way of example, he was not impressed with Michel Barnier, and thinks it strange that someone who has no experience of financial services has the regulation of the UK's most important industry in his hands.

Equally, the FSA's resistance to publishing their insights into the failure of RBS was a mistake, and for Lord Turner to only publish the report with the permission of Stephen Hester is a sign of weakness.

Andrew then went on to talk around the Parliamentary Houses a little about how getting the country straight hasn't even started yet and that their biggest challenge will be trust in their ability to reform. Like many of our generation, Andrew grew up as a Thatcherite youth, in his case a Conservative one, and so he claimed that you may not have liked Thatcher's reforms but did you trust her to get them through? Yes.

The challenge today is that after the Iraq War and the Parliamentary expenses scandal, does anyone trust the politicians today to reform effectively? No. This is their biggest challenge and, funnily enough, the number of times I hear about 'rebuilding trust' in banking, it's common to both politics and finance. There again, politics and finance are near enough the same thing these days, aren't they?

Further to this general introduction, Andrew went on to talk about regulatory reform in the finance sector and made clear that, although banker bashing is popular amongst the public and the media, it wasn't just banks that failed and it wasn't just banks that cause this crisis. Everyone had a hand in the crisis from the Prime Minister and Chancellor to the Governor of the Bank of England to the Financial Services Authority (FSA), ratings agencies, auditors, the boards of banks and their chief executives. Even the consumers who over-mortgaged and the businesses that over-borrowed are to blame for some part of this crisis. [Note: there was an audible sense of disagreement amongst some of the audience when this comment was made.]

What Andrew was really getting at is that all of the parties involved in organising, regulating, managing and running the financial system overlooked the growth of risk on the balance sheet of the banks, and this is where future regulations need to focus.

On this note, he did not think the Dodd-Frank regulation addressed the issues above. Instead it merely presents the problem and leaves it to the regulators to sort it out.

Funnily enough, the solution here is expected to come out of the Independent Commission on Banking (ICB). However, after my attendance the night before at their hearing, I don't think so.

All in all, I agreed with much of what Andrew covered and said. He's a realist.

He does not believe that regulation will solve anything – has Basel ever achieved anything? – and that the more regulation is put into place, the more it costs the customers to fund its implementation.

This is all true. Equally, the business cycle of finance is endemic, and so there will be another crash in the future. In fact, many of us think it's already bubbling away in China.

So what is the answer? No regulations at all? Or 100% regulations written for every possible nuance and avenue of running a bank? The former is the Wild West and the latter is boa constriction. The balance has to be somewhere in the middle, and that's what the Treasury Select Committee, the Independent Commission on Banking, the Chancellor, the Bank and the FSA are all trying to achieve.

Mind you, isn't that what they were trying to achieve before this crisis hit?

What is this f****r fee? (2010)

So yesterday's big news is the new Financial Crisis Responsibility Fee, the FCR, or f****r fee, as the bankers are calling it. This is Obama's big idea to get back lost TARP funds, by introducing a tax of $1.5 million per billion dollars of liabilities on a bank's balance sheet.

The aim is to raise $117 billion to make up for the losses during the financial crisis. The way it will work is that the banks pay this 0.15% on liabilities and, according to Goldman Sachs, there are around $5.5 trillion of liabilities on American banks' balance sheets, so that's around $8 billion per year. The tax will apply for 10 years, until 2020, or until the TARP fund losses are repaid.

The fee will be applied to only the largest banks, those with more than $50 billion worth of assets, and 60% of the tax will be paid for by the largest banks: JPMorgan, Citi, Bank of America, Wells Fargo, Goldman and co. In fact, the biggest banks will be paying about $2 billion a year for this tax.

There's also about $1 billion a year that will be paid by UK banks Royal Bank of Scotland (which owns Citizens and Charter One Banks), HSBC (which owns Household) and Barclays (which bought the US operations of Lehmans).

Sounds bad, but it's not so bad. US banks made $250 billion in earnings last year, so paying back up to $10 billion a year in tax ain't so bad. In fact, I was amazed to find a figure that states that Goldman Sachs made $100 million a day in earnings last year every day for over 200 trading days. So a billion here or there in taxes ain't so bad, especially if you're paying billions in bonuses and annoying everyone.

The FCR fee is stirring stuff therefore, and very populist as it ensures that Barack Obama "recovers every single dime the American people are owed", and hits at the heart of the anger everyone has with bankers making "massive profits and obscene bonuses".

In some ways, it's a good idea. It targets leverage and borrowings that banks tap into in the wholesale markets, which is where Lehman and Northern Rock got scuppered and where Goldman Sachs and Morgan Stanley plough their trough.

The FCR fee also positions itself as the insurance fee which the banks should have paid to get themselves bailed out. They didn't pay any insurance but then found they were too big to fail so the Fed insured them. This is now payback time.

But it won't work. First, it hits at the banks, but the banks have paid back TARP. $165 billion of TARP funds were repaid by US banks last year, with an average return to the US taxpayer of an 8% yield. That's why the Fed made a $45 billion profit last year, through bond purchases and interest on the emergency loans made to financial institutions. It was General Motors, Chrysler and AIG that lost the $120 billion of funds that Obama wants to recoup.

Second, the banks will just pass on the cost of the tax to their customers and investors. Jamie Dimon, CEO of JPMorgan, made the comment straight off that "all businesses pass costs on to customers", and it is highly likely that the banks will find some way to hide this tax in the costs of doing business. The result is that the proposed tax will be rejected by Congress, which sees any tax on the taxpayer as being untenable. The tax has to be directly on the bank.

Third, Geithner ruled out a Tobin tax on bank transactions at the G20 Finance Ministers summit in Gleneagles last November for the reasons outlined in point two above. The trouble is that the FCR fee is a variation of a Tobin tax and needs to be better thought out. Obama had and has until 2013 to find a way to get the lost TARP funds repaid, and so he doesn't need to do something this fast or ill-conceived.

Finally, this does not address the two biggest issues: bankers' bonuses and being too big to fail. Obama claims it gets at "massive profits and obscene bonuses" ... how? I don't see it.

If these are the major issues that lie at the heart of the post-crisis bubble of media and public bile, then these need to be addressed, but the FCR fee doesn't do it. The FCR fee purely repays TARP.

In fact, if bonuses and too big to fail are the core issues then these issues need to be addressed through a G20 agenda, not a unilateralist position, whether it be in the UK, USA, France or elsewhere.

Therefore, it is far more likely that the FCR fee will be rejected by Congress and Geithner and Obama end up working with Barnier, Darling, Brown, Sarkozy and company on clawbacks and taxes on banker's bonuses, along with a variation of Glass-Steagall to bring back a return to 'narrow banking'. In other words, split the risky investment markets from the retail depositors.

This last point is the key act forecast to happen over the next year or so, and is far more likely to be operable and implementable than a FCR fee.

Gordon Brown's Tobin tax ... duh? (2009)

Many of us thought it a bit weird that Gordon Brown suggested bringing back the Tobin tax last weekend during the G20 summit. The idea is to tax every financial transaction, just a little bit, one or two cents on each ... this way you can build up a fund for any future financial shocks.

The reason it's a bit weird is that any action by governments need to be co-ordinated across all G20 nations – unilateral activities will just cause banks to relocate elsewhere – and Gordon had zero support for this idea from his usually supportive key allies.

As with the bank bonuses debate, the issue of unilateral versus collective responsibility is a big concern and is why the UK and USA have been acting in close harmony, like Siamese twins, during this crisis to make sure they're co-ordinated in all announcements.

So it was very strange that Brown would suggest the Tobin tax when Tim Geithner came out five minutes later, saying that it was not something the US would consider.

But what was even weirder, as pointed out by *Private Eye* this week, is that the government and Gordon Brown have consistently rejected the idea of a Tobin tax for the past decade.

For example, in May 2002 when Gordon Brown was Chancellor, he made this statement to the Parliamentary Committee for International Development:

> "The problem is that each of the other proposals, like the Tobin tax ... has very substantial drawbacks and they have failed to command the international support that is necessary for us to raise the level of finance over a short period of time so that we can achieve the Millennium Development Goals."

The rich vein of anti-Tobin views continues through the ensuing years as, just last December, Gordon Brown was asked in Prime Minister's Questions whether he would support such a tax:

> "There are many proposals to deal with the reform of international financial institutions to make them more able to deal with the problems that the world faces, not just the financial stability problems, but climate change. One such proposal is the Tobin tax, which has been found by many people who have looked at it not to be implementable."

Even in August, when Lord Turner of the FSA mentioned the idea, it was pooh-poohed by the Chancellor. Nevertheless, this was the same dialogue by Lord Turner where he used the phrase "socially useless". Ever since, we've all been wondering what role for the future for banks in society, and the idea of bringing back the Tobin tax on financial transactions has obviously seeped into Brown's armoury.

So maybe Lord Turner has convinced him to make a U-turn on Britain's anti-Tobin tax feelings. Now, there's no reason why a politician shouldn't do a U-turn. It doesn't look good but, bear in mind that back in 2002-2003, Gordon Brown also refused to believe there was a credit bubble burgeoning in Britain.

(...)

Times have changed and obviously Gordon Brown is not a soothsayer or Nostradamus or Warren Buffett ... and so he might be right in performing a U-turn on this tax on transactions. The only mistake he made was not running this past the Americans (and Canadians, Russians and IMF) beforehand as they all rejected it out of hand, as he probably knew they would.

If you ask me it was just a cunning plan, to get more support for Tony Blair in the new EU roles of European President. After all, the Tobin tax is specifically supported and promoted by the French and Germans. Showing support of their policies may well be a political play that Gordon thought a good one.

Why the G20 will disagree with the IMF reforms (2010)

I don't know if any of you read the IMF report recommending two new bank taxes:

◆ A bank levy based upon the risk banks represent, called a Financial Stability Contribution (FSC); and

◆ A straight tax on profits and bonuses called the Financial Activities Tax (FAT).

If you haven't, then I can recommend it's worth a skim. For example, they reject the Tobin tax / Robin Hood tax idea, saying that this would just get passed on to customers by the banks.

However, the fact that they support the idea of a levy and a tax – a double whammy – could have bankers worried ... except that bankers are pretty clever at tax avoidance and Canada and Japan have said they won't implement these plans so it's a G18 agreement right now, or less.

In my view, the document is also flawed. Here's why.

The document itself is just for discussion for the G20 Ministers meeting this week, with the aim of agreeing something in June. But it does contain some really interesting appendices which are noteworthy as useful research materials, covering diverse subjects from each country's proposals for reform to their contributions to the bank crisis to date.

For example, the table that follows shows the amounts announced or pledged for financial sector support so far, as a percentage of 2009's GDP.

	Capital Injection	Purchase of Assets and Lending by Treasury	Direct Support	Guarantees	Asset Swap and Purchase of Financial Assets, including Treasuries, by Central Bank	Upfront Government Financing
	(A)	(B)	(A+B)	(C)	(D)	(E)
G-20 Average	**2.6**	**1.4**	**4.0**	**6.4**	**4.6**	**3.1**
Advanced Economies	3.8	2.4	6.2	13.2	7.7	5.0
in billions of US$	1,220	756	1,976	3.530	2.400	1,610
Emerging Economies	0.7	0.1	0.8	16.9	0.0	0.2
in billions of US$	90	18	108	7	0	24

2 : Governments in action

What this shows is that for the 'advanced economies' – think USA, UK, France, Germany, Japan et al – the cost has been 6.2% of GDP in direct support and a further 10.9% in guarantees. The total of columns A to E represents 29.8% of advanced economies' GDP in 2009. That compares with 1.8% in the emerging economies – think the BRICs, Indonesia, et al.

Mind you, they then go on to say that "for the advanced G-20 economies, the average amount utilized for capital injection was 2 percent of GDP, that is $639 billion, or just over half the pledged amounts. France, Germany, the USA and the UK accounted for over 90 percent of this. For the advanced G-20 economies, the utilized amount for asset purchases was around 1.4 percent of GDP, less than two-thirds of the pledged amount. Similarly, the uptake of guarantees has been markedly less than pledged."

This is why the report reckons that the global financial crisis has cost about $533 billion less than originally estimated, and is now just a mere $2.28 trillion when all is said and done.

Now, who's the daddy when it comes to global bailouts and guarantees? Have a look at the next table.

The Extraordinary Madness of Banks and the
Extreme Folly of Governments

	Capital Injection	Purchase of Assets and Lending by Treasury 2/	Direct Support 3/	Guarantees 4/	Asset Swap and Purchase of Financial Assets, including Treasuries, by Central Bank	Upfront Government Financing 5/
	(A)	(B)	(A+B)	(C)	(D)	(E)
Advanced Economies						
Australia	0.0	0.0	0.0	13.2	0.0	0.0
Canada	0.0	9.1	9.1	0.0	0.0	9.1
France	1.3	0.2	1.5	16.9	0.0	1.1
Germany	3.4	0.0	3.4	17.2	0.0	3.4
Italy	1.3	0.0	1.3	0.0	2.7	2.7
Japan	2.5	4.1	6.6	7.2	0.0	0.4
Korea	1.2	1.5	2.7	11.6	0.0	0.8
United Kingdom	8.2	3.7	11.9	40.0	28.2	8.7
United States	5.1	2.3	7.4	7.5	12.1	7.4

Wow, the UK wins! We're number one, we're number one, we're number one, woohoohoo!.

Wait a minute. That means we're #1 in global bailouts of banks. Hmmm ... not sure if we should be so thrilled with that accolade and maybe this is why Gordon Brown is so keen on the idea of a Tobin tax or a Robin Hood tax or a Financial Activities tax or ... well, any tax really to help with our debt mountain, to be honest. The burden of national debt amongst the G7 nations is at a 60-year high, with the UK's Treasury planning to increase national debt by over £560 billion between now and 2015. That's about $800 billion or almost a trillion.

Meanwhile, the emerging economies paint a very different picture, as shown in the next table.

The Extraordinary Madness of Banks and the
Extreme Folly of Governments

	Capital Injection	Purchase of Assets and Lending by Treasury 2/	Direct Support 3/	Guarantees 4/	Asset Swap and Purchase of Financial Assets, including Treasuries, by Central Bank	Upfront Government Financing 5/
	(A)	(B)	(A+B)	(C)	(D)	(E)
Emerging Economies						
Argentina	0.0	0.0	0.0	0.0	0.0	0.0
Brazil	0.0	0.8	0.0	0.5	0.0	0.0
China	0.0	0.0	0.0	0.0	0.0	0.0
India	0.0	0.0	0.0	0.0	0.0	0.0
Indonesia	0.0	0.0	0.0	0.0	0.0	0.0
Mexico	0.0	0.0	0.0	0.0	0.0	0.0
Russia	7.1	0.5	7.7	0.0	0.0	1.9
Saudi Arabia	0.0	0.0	0.0	0.0	0.0	0.0
South Africa	0.0	0.0	0.0	0.0	0.0	0.0
Turkey	0.0	0.0	0.0	0.0	0.0	0.0

Apart from Russia, this crisis has cost the key future economies of the world urrmmmm ... nothing.

These charts make it clear that **nine** of the G20 nations have had no crisis. Add to this the fact that Canada's financial system has been the most stable in the world, and Japan does not intend to implement these tax and levy options, and you realise that under half of the G20 will be keen to support any radical changes to the financial markets.

It's not as clear-cut as this, as the fact that the advanced economies' bailouts allowed the emerging economies to survive this crisis without their economies also imploding is a key part of the dialogue.

Another useful chart (see over) shows why the IMF has reduced the bailout numbers by $533 billion where financial markets have used far less of the pledged amounts than those offered by their respective governments:

	Capital Injection		Purchase of Assets and Lending by Treasury 2/	
	Amount used	In percent of announcement	Amount used	In percent of announcement
Advanced Economies				
Australia	0.0	...	0.0	...
Canada	0.0	...	83.2	48.4
France	1.1	83.2	0.0	0.0
Germany	1.2	35.0	83.2	...
Italy	0.3	20.3	0.0	...
Japan	0.1	2.4	0.1	1.4
Korea	0.4	32.5	0.1	3.8
United Kingdom	6.4	78.5	0.1	4.0
United States	2.9	57.0	1.9	84.0
Emerging Economies				
Argentina	0.0	...	0.0	...
Brazil	0.0	...	0.3	43.5
China	0.0	...	0.0	...
India	0.0	...	0.0	...
Indonesia	0.0	...	0.0	...
Mexico	0.0	...	0.0	...
Russia	3.1	43.0	0.0	0.0
Saudi Arabia	0.0	...	0.0	...
South Africa	0.0	...	0.0	...
Turkey	0.0	...	0.0	...
G-20 Average	1.3	51.7	0.9	60.2
Advanced Economies	2.0	52.3	1.4	61.0
in billions of US$	639	...	461	...
Emerging Economies	0.3	43.0	0.03	27.5
in billions of US$	38.4	...	5.0	...

Finally, these charts are followed by a review of each country's bank taxation policies implemented or proposed (Appendix 2, Page 32), a review of corrective taxation and prudential policies (Appendix 3) and the current taxation policies (Appendix 4).

This last section is also particularly intriguing as it demonstrates why banking has been so critical to Gordon Brown's policies of the past decade. For example, here's the percentage of a country's total tax pool raised from financial firms by country.

G20 corporate taxes paid by the financial sector (%)

	Period	Share of Corporate Taxes	Share of Total Tax Revenue
Argentina	2006 – 2008	6.0	1.0
Australia	FY2007	15.0	2.8
Brazil	2006 – 2008	15.4	1.8
Canada	2006 – 2007	23.5	2.6
China			
France	2006 – 2008	18.0	1.9
Germany			
India			
Indonesia			
Italy	2006 – 2008	26.3	1.7
Japan			
Mexico 1/	2006 – 2008	11.2	3.1
Russia			
Saudi Arabia			
South Africa	2007 – 2008 FY	13.7	3.5
South Korea	2006 – 2008	17.7	3.0
Turkey	2006 – 2008 FY	23.6	2.1
United Kingdom	2006 – 2008 FY	20.9	1.9
United States	2006 – 2007 FY	18.2	1.9
Unweighted Average		17.5	2.3
Source: IMF Staff estimates based on G-20 survey. 1/ Shares of nonoil CIT revenue and total nonoil tax revenue.			

67

This makes it clear that for every country, but particularly for Italy, Turkey, Canada and the UK, the role and influence of the financial sectors on their economies and government policies is fundamental to the country and its economic and public sector health.

Without bank taxes, countries fail. But with bank failures, countries fail. And that is their Catch-22 and the reason why this is so hard to change.

Between domestic interests and focus, aligned with the radically different ways in which this crisis has impacted each G20 nation, it is unlikely that we shall ever see a simple agreement of policy reform now, or at the G20 meeting in Toronto in June.

The G20 party is over … or is it? (2009)

So the G20 meeting is over and has an agreement to spend over $1 trillion through the IMF on nations that are worthy. The other key agreements include:

◆ A lockdown on the tax regimes of countries where people hide place their wealth. The age of bank 'secrecy' is over they say, although I'm not sure that Switzerland, the Caymans and other nations will appreciate that very much. Mind you, the OECD has just listed the tax havens they views as uncooperative, with Costa Rica, Malaysia (Labuan), the Philippines and Uruguay singled out as "jurisdictions that have not committed to the internationally agreed tax standard";

◆ A crackdown on light touch regulation and particularly on hedge funds, credit rating agencies and the operations of banks in the Over-the-Counter, or 'shadow' banking markets;

- The creation of a new Financial Stability Board, which will focus upon financial stability across all major economies; and
- Measures to address the issues in the banking system by preventing excessive leverage and forcing banks to have higher reserve policies so that we avoid being left under-capitalised in a downturn again.

There's a lot more to it, but I guess the key implications for banks are that there will be a fundamental rethinking of core products and services as:

- All systemically important financial institutions will be covered by the rules, including hedge funds;
- Capital requirements will change provisioning, and this may lead to a new Basel III;
- The current Financial Stability Forum becomes the Financial Stability Board and will embrace all G20 countries, the European Commission and Spain;
- The new Board will have a much wider mandate to promote financial stability, set financial guidelines and monitor supervisors for the major cross-border institutions; and
- Challenges in using cross-border tax loopholes for profits and products.

On the last one, I just realised something. One of my bank friends works in London two to three days a week, but lives in a tax haven called Monaco to escape tax here. Surely now, he'll move to Costa Rica. Nice weather, and no pressure from the G20 on his tax.

Maybe they should register the bank's head office there too?

Anyway, the G20 Summit was a useful step forward as it gathered clarity from the world's largest nations in stemming this crisis and moving forward. It was useful, even though all of the agreements were made beforehand by the civil servants.

Chapter 3 Regulators' reaction

Introduction

Once the politicians have sorted out their act, the next group to rally to action are the regulators. Interestingly, the regulators that everyone looked towards for leadership – the Federal Reserve and Securities and Exchange Commission (SEC) in the USA, and the Financial Services Authority (FSA) and Bank of England in the UK – were the same regulators who were being lambasted by all for their failure to supervise. This has resulted in significant restructuring of bank supervision and yet, for all their failings, it was and is the regulators who have to make banks work. This is because the role of the regulator is to create rules and, more importantly, to enforce them. And some might say that it was the failure of enforcement rather than regulation that caused the issues we faced at the end of the last decade. Or maybe it was both ...

Bickers over Vickers: the right stuff? (2011)

So the Vickers Report has finally crept out into the wilderness. All 358 pages of it. Half of it talks about how to increase the competitiveness of banking and the other half about what to do if a bank fails in another crisis.

The latter has garnered all the news headlines, whist the former has been generally overlooked.

More copy has been written about this report than anything else in banking over the past week or so, with a selection of headlines that makes the mind reel.

Here's a summary of the key points on ring-fencing:

- ◆ Ring-fencing is confirmed, where banks separate domestic retail banking services from global wholesale/investment banking. The commission is vague about whether banking to large companies should be in or outside the ring-fence but it suggests that between one-sixth and a third of the £6 trillion of bank assets should be inside the ring-fence.

◆ The ICB describes the ring-fence as "high" and said that the ring-fenced part of the bank should have its own board and be legally and operationally separate from the parent bank.

◆ Ring-fenced banks should have a capital cushion of up to 20% comprising equity of 10%, with an extra amount of other capital such as bonds. The largest ring-fenced banks should have at least 17% of equity and bonds, and a further loss-absorbing buffer of up to 3% if "the supervisor has concerns about their ability to be resolved without cost to the taxpayer".

◆ Capital could be moved from the ring-fenced bank to the investment bank, as long as the capital ratio of the ring-fenced bank did not fall below the 10% minimum.

And on creating new competition:

◆ The ICB has backtracked on an idea in its interim report that Lloyds Banking Group be required to sell off more than the 632 branches it currently has on the market to meet EU rules on state aid. It dilutes this, to say that it "recommends that the government seek agreement with Lloyds Banking Group to ensure that the divesture leads to the emergence of a strong challenger bank."

◆ It should be easier to switch bank accounts and the ICB recommends "the early introduction" of a system that makes it easier to move accounts and that is "free of risk and cost to customers". It rules out number portability – as is used with mobile phones – in favour of this switching service. The amount of interest that customers miss out on by having a current account – known as interest fore-gone – should also be published on annual statements.

◆ The industry should be referred for a competition investigation in 2015.

For the most part, I'm disappointed with this report. It's not that I'm against bank reform, but what is the right sort of bank reform? What this report appears to do is tread a fine line between bank anger, government need and public input, and comes out on the side of muddle.

It's already had plenty of flak for this, but let's pick on a couple of things.

First, account portability. Why hasn't the ICB included this, as it makes eminent sense as discussed back in December at the ICB meeting I attended.

What the report actually says about this is as follows:

> "The Commission recommends the early introduction of a redirection service for personal and SME current accounts (to make account switching easier) which, among other things, transfers accounts within seven working days, provides seamless redirection for more than a year, and is free of risk and cost to customers. This should boost confidence in the ease of switching and enhance the competitive pressure exerted on banks through customer choice. The Commission has considered recommending account number portability. For now, it appears that its costs and incremental benefits are uncertain relative to redirection, but that may change in the future."

In other words, the cost of using different account numbers between banks allowing portability is too great. For example, if might from RBS to Lloyds with account number 75280025, there may already be someone at Lloyds with that account number. Therefore, to introduce account portability of account numbers, you would probably need to renumber all the bank accounts in Britain with unique IDs. That's why it's been dropped.

But then the report adds more details to this idea (page 218) and shows it is feasible:

> "Under account number portability, a customer's sort code and account number would not change when the customer changed banks, thereby avoiding the need to change any payment or credit instructions. Evidence to the Commission suggested that the effect of account number portability could be achieved through the creation of an 'alias database'. This proposal is for a new database to be created with a new code for each account that would be assigned to each sort code and account number: a customer would give the direct debit originators (and creditors) they deal with the new code, which would never change; when the customer moved banks, the sort code and account number assigned to the customer's code would change and nothing else."

Later on (page 222), it expands on the risks and opportunities of account portability:

> "One significant benefit of account number portability (whether done through making existing account numbers effectively portable, or through the creation of an alias database) is that it would remove the cost of switching to direct debit originators, as well as those who make automatic payments into customers' accounts. However, given the importance of the payments system, it would be critical to ensure that the migration to account number portability did not disrupt the flow of payments or introduce greater operational risks into the payments system."

In light of a need for bank reform, this would have been a worthwhile aspect to develop now, and it is something left in the report for further evaluation so you never know.

The Extraordinary Madness of Banks and the
Extreme Folly of Governments

Nevertheless, the big question is whether this would improve competition anyway?

Competition is more about the barriers to entry – governance, licensing, capital, technology etc – and hence, these are more mighty areas … that the report also fails to address.

The report mentions competition 414 times, and yet the main recommendations of the interim report:

♦ "that the divestiture of Lloyds' assets and liabilities required for EU state aid approval will have a limited effect on competition unless it is substantially enhanced;

♦ "that it may be possible to introduce greatly improved means of switching at reasonable cost, and to improve transparency; and

♦ "that the new Financial Conduct Authority (FCA) should have a clear primary duty to promote effective competition";

… have all been watered down.

Then we move onto ring-fencing, which purely addresses the aspects of what to do if a bank fails.

> "Structural separation should make it easier and less costly to resolve banks that get into trouble. By 'resolution' is meant an orderly process to determine which activities of a failing bank are to be continued and how. Depending on the circumstances, different solutions may be appropriate for different activities. For example, some activities might be wound down, some sold to other market participants, and others formed into a 'bridge bank' under new management, their shareholders and creditors having been wiped out in whole and/or part. Orderliness involves averting contagion, avoiding taxpayer liability, and ensuring the continuous provision of necessary retail banking services – as distinct from entire

banks – for which customers have no ready alternatives. Separation would allow better-targeted policies towards banks in difficulty, and would minimise the need for support from the taxpayer. One of the key benefits of separation is that it would make it easier for the authorities to require creditors of failing retail banks, failing wholesale/investment banks, or both, if necessary, to bear losses, instead of the taxpayer."

Living wills and all that aside, the proposal to leave banks as integrated universal operators – good for Barclays – by purely creating a delineation between their domestic commercial and retail banking operations versus their global links is a duck out.

Why? Because it does not address the issue of why banks fail, but just what to do when they fail. This is a positive thing according to some and yes, sure, it's a good thing to know what to do when a bank fails ... but why not try to deal with the core of failure as, even if we know what to do, a bank failure in its investment arm will still destroy value in its overall operations.

Northern Rock illustrates this well where, as a pure retail bank, it failed due to securitising its loans and mortgages in the wholesale markets. Surely these aspects of potential liquidity failure should have been in the report, and how a bank builds an illiquid position that leads to failure, rather than just what to do post the event.

And no, I'm not forgetting that through a ring-fence recommendation increased capitalisation of both the retail and investment operations will help, but an illiquid position is still on the cards and that is surely a point that should have been the core of the reforms, not the post-failure fall out?

Equally as Sir John Vickers has been saying: "The too big to fail problem must not be recast as a too delicate to reform problem", but is he reforming or just adding insult to injury? As the action of ring fencing is a unilateral action not being followed by any other major nation right now, it may be the latter.

77

Renowned former Federal Reserve Chairman Paul Volcker gets to the heart of the matter when he says that he "completely doesn't understand the British approach, where they can leave all these questions unanswered. They said they wanted a retail bank in the same holding company as everything else. I don't know what 'everything else' means. Is that not a bank too? It's just a wholesale bank. Who makes the payment system work – the retail bank or the wholesale bank ... the philosophy is you are a group of banks that serve the consumers, the retail customer, and that hold their deposits with the central bank and so forth, does not solve the problem with all the other parts of the financial system. I also don't believe in a firewall or Chinese wall between them, as you need a very high ring fence to stop the deer jumping over."

Sir John may claim the fence is high, but it cannot be high enough.

When a Barclays investment bank fails, it will still bring down Barclays Bank as Barclays investment banking operations represents 42% of the bank's total revenues (Royal Bank of Scotland generates a third of all revenues from investment operations; HSBC 27%; and Lloyds Banking Group is uncertain as it has no official investment banking arm).

Meanwhile, the costs are at least £4 billion to implement these reforms and the overall programme has really hammered the value of the UK banking sector in the world's financial markets, with much of the loss of value this year due to Sir John's committee's actions combined with the Eurozone crisis.

So my key question is that we are living in a world where Basel III, G20 reform, European Union Directives along with American restructuring is creating so much imbalance in the global financial system that adding to such imbalance though unilateral action is questionable.

All in all, the whole area is a cauldron of trouble and messiness that this report has done little to resolve and, if anything, has fuelled more debate about the UK's sole stance in the face of global regulatory drives.

So what should we do? We should ensure that we work in harmony with Wall Street on the capital market reforms whilst implementing domestic policies to lower the barriers to entry for new entrants in banking.

The former may be seen as being difficult, but the #1 objective of the UK should be to maintain UK's attractiveness as a centre for financial services.

That's the piece that has been most badly damaged by these proposed reforms.

Luckily, it won't be implemented until 2019 in order to ensure consistency with the developments of Basel III, so delay was inevitable after all.

Fall-out from the flash crash (2011)

Another presentation at TradeTech that I was interested to hear was Larry Tabb's. Larry is CEO of TABB Group, a research firm focused on capital markets that Larry founded in 2003 after several years leading TowerGroup's Securities & Investments Practice.

Due to our involvement in TowerGroup – I co-created TowerGroup Europe – Larry's one of the interesting guys for me, as he has grown his firm to around 30 people today and has a strong knowledge of all things in the investment markets.

So what was he talking about? The flash crash, a subject I've blogged about extensively. Larry has spent some time on the subject and forensically analyses it in depth in various research.

As we all now know, the flash crash began when one mutual fund group, Waddell & Reed, put in a large sell order for eMini futures. This was on May 6th 2010 and it is important to remember that this was when there was a lot of economic uncertainty, with Greece causing a lot of nerves in the markets.

Larry reckons that Waddell & Reed put in a sell order for 75,000 eMini contracts worth over $4 billion at 14:32 that day through their algorithmic trading machines.

The result was that Liquidity Replenishment Points (LRP) kicked into the NYSE index as algos started selling massively with other algos, and high frequency trading (HFT) systems were trading futures and eMinis among themselves looking for any systems out there that would trade. Internaliser engines stopped trading and stub quotes – absurdly priced quotes that acts as placeholders when trading firms don't want to trade – were being issued for a cent each.

By 15:00, over two billion shares were being traded during a ten-minute period. Normally, you wouldn't see that sort of volume of trading in a whole day.

Making matters worse, FINRA cancelled most of the trades that were placed at that time, describing them as 'erroneous', causing a huge reconciliations backlog of work.

What a mess.

Since the flash crash, the markets have seen some activity picking up to regulate this.

There are short-selling limits, circuit breakers and a tightening of market thresholds on NYSE and NASDAQ. There's some other ideas about circuit breaker rules for limit up and limit down to ensure that trades are only executed within a range tied to recent prices for a security, as well as other direct access rules.

What was more interesting in Larry's presentation is what's also under discussion.

For example, having the algorithms used by trading firms checked and vetted by a competent authority or regulator.

◆   How do you define what is an algorithm?

- Do the authorities have the resources to fully investigate such systems?
- Do they have the competence?

There's a view that 'time in force' rules need to be introduced for non-market makers. This rule ensures that buy orders stay in the markets long enough to be filled, as many buy orders are used to potentially lift prices using 'flash orders'. Flash orders appear in a short burst and are cancelled just as fast in order to change prices on exchange to the traders' favour. Hence, the idea of flash orders causing the flash crash is in the regulator's heads.

However, this rule is viewed as inappropriate by the markets, as exchanges queue orders at their servers and process them sequentially. Therefore, cancelled orders pose no threat to the exchanges. In particular, time in force is a problem as it would allow market makers to pick off the non-market makers and get market gains as a result.

There are other views in this area also, such as reallocating the cost of market infrastructure based upon order cancellation rates on a pro rata across trading firms. Again, sounds good in principle, but any reallocation of costs will simply get passed through to clients, so that's not good either.

There's also a long discussion about an SEC Consolidated Audit Trial. The Consolidated Audit Trial should allow regulators to track information related to orders received and executed across the securities markets and, similar to the FSA's view, should allow date-time stamping and order flow to be monitored and audited.

This sounds good in principle, although Tabb estimates that this will cost over $4 billion to build and $2 billion per annum to maintain. Sounds costly.

Finally, things like a Central Limit Order Book (CLOB), a ban on stub quotes and concentration rules to bring order flow back onto exchanges are all being mooted.

All of these have issues, particularly the last which has not only been eradicated in Europe recently (MiFID reversed the national exchanges' 'concentration rule') but it also would force orders from dark pools into lit markets. That's not good for liquidity.

So what should be done? Larry split this into four buckets.

First, the easy stuff such as co-ordinated circuit breakers. This is a good move as part of the flash crash issue was uncoordinated markets. As the flash crash began, CME hit the circuit breakers but NYSE hit the LRPs. This meant that CME indexed products stopped trading, but cash products carried on, so while NYSE stopped trading in the cash markets, other markets didn't. Co-ordinated market breakers is an easy thing to bring in under regulatory process as it would just ensure all markets are consistent in approach.

Slightly harder but do-able is the Consolidated Audit Trail, already discussed. Add onto this an increase in collateral held with the CCP for HFT firms, new pre-trade and post-trade risk rules, and this may all help.

Tabb sees it as being really harder to do things like CLOB, which is probably why this has been discussed for over a decade but still not happening.

And it is impossible and undesirable to even think of going down the route of algo vetting or introducing market maker incentives, transaction taxes or other rules, according to Tabb.

All in all, a great overview of a complex subject and something that is still under wide debate across the industry. It will be interesting to see how the debate concludes and, going back to my regulatory DUPE discussion, how the market is squeezed and the resultant bubble that forms.

Review: The Independent Commission on Banking Interim Report ** (April 2011)

** out of a possible *****

And so the long-awaited Independent Commission on Banking (ICB) produced its report yesterday, and we all went … hmmmm.

Me? I think it's a political compromise that assuages the banks whilst showing the governments trying to force a strong hand, when it doesn't have one.

In essence, after a nine-month long gestation period, the report is like a pregnant pause. A moment of held breath that, when you release it, shows there was just a silent moment with little changed.

The report does have some good things in it, like the idea that banks should be fire-walled to allow the bit that can fail to do just that, but the overall view has to be that it's just BAU (Banking As Usual).

Barclays share price bounced strongly upwards having dropped heavily last week. This was due to the expectation that prop trading, the Volcker Rule and even a return to Glass-Steagall would be incorporated in the ICB's report, leading to a break-up of the bank.

That hasn't happened. What happened instead is that the banks have been told that they must ring-fence the risky bits of banking – trading and investing – from the bits that need to be safe – retail and commercial. This is so that if the risky bits fail in the future, they can be allowed to without impacting the safe bits.

I see it as like separating the jungle from the farm. The jungle is the investment bank; the farm is the retail bank. The jungle is full of dangerous animals that can kill you; the farm is full of nice things, like chickens and cows, which you control. The jungle is full of risk and excitement and, if you come out the other end intact, you can reap big rewards; the farm is open and easy, with everything under control and reliable results the expectation.

What we had before is a single landscape within a bank – a Universal Bank – where the jungle and the farm existed on the same plateau. Hence, when the jungle went out of control, the wild animals ate all the ones we were trying to nurture for sustenance, and the whole bank failed.

Under the ICB's report, the two must now be kept distinctly different. Therefore, two separate plateaus and a big chasm – or firewall – in between.

It sounds ok in theory. It doesn't go as far as Glass-Steagall, but it does go to the extent of making clear that if the jungle catches fire, then the farm is easy to save. But that's got nothing to do with long-term bank stability.

HBOS was a farm. Northern Rock was a farm. They both burnt down due to using the jungle for support and leverage. Under the ICB view of the world, these farms would be safer because they would not leverage or use the jungle in quite the same way; and they would have far more capital in reserve, should the occasion arise, to survive a meltdown.

That cost of capital reserving will add about £5 billion to the bill for banking according to the FT, or even more than double that according to Oliver Wyman, which is why costs to customers will increase.

Meanwhile, the idea that the ICB has stimulated competition by making accounts easier to switch and telling Lloyds Banking Group to shrink further is also contestable. Customers don't switch accounts today. Is that because it's hard, or because there's no reason to bother? Does the report make it easier for new banks, like Metro Bank, to launch? Will a smaller Lloyds be any different to a bigger Lloyds? Does it really make the banking world better?

Probably not. That's why I said last week that the Treasury Select Committee (TSC) had laid a bomb for the ICB. In that blog entry, TSC member John Mann called it "a whitewash", published with conclusions made by "a bunch of elites coming up with something palatable to banks."

Many would say he's right, but then what can the ICB and Chancellor do? Be radical and lose the banks support for the UK completely? Lose all those tax pounds and pence?

No. So the result is that Lloyds are a bit miffed as they are the target of being too big to retail, whilst the rest are fed up that Barclays has won the day.

For me, it was just another day in the jungle.

Watch your back.

The future of banking regulation (2010)

The City of London released an interesting document yesterday on the future of regulation of banking. They talk about liquidity, leverage, capital and risk liberally, and state that the future regulatory regime must not clamp down on capital reserves in banking so hard that the banks are unable to lubricate the global economy.

What I found interesting is that there are quite a few contradictions in the 77-page report although, to be honest, I only read the Executive Summary.

From this summary, it's interesting that they plead that the macroprudential structures don't squeeze capital ratios, but hardly talk at all about the leverage issues Lehman Brothers created.

If my memory serves me, Lehman was operating at leverage ratios of up to 1:40, e.g. for every $1 of capital, $40 was being used to 'gamble' on the global markets. I also remember that their debts at bankruptcy were around $400 billion and BarCap estimated that for every $1 of debt, around $20 of CDS were being leveraged against Lehman's AAA rating. In other words, $8 trillion of leverage was in the system off the back of Lehman Brothers.

That was the issue, particularly when this leverage – and therefore liquidity – disappeared overnight.

Following on from this, they refer to the fact that the crisis was not caused by a lack of capital, but by a lack of liquidity. True, but I did not gather a clear view on liquidity risk or leverage ratios from the document. It may be in there, but it's hard to find.

For example, in Section Five that addresses leverage ratios, the report states that: "Judgement and discretion are vital, including judgement and discretion concerning circumstances under which firms will be permitted temporarily to have capital that is inadequate. The notion of employing a leverage ratio as a last-resort backstop to limit the damage caused by regulatory get-arounds arises precisely because of the limited ability and appetite of regulatory authorities for exercising discretion. That core problem is the one to address."

A bit of fudge there, if you ask me.

The same is true on liquidity risk, with the report proposing a global liquidity standard and yet they then say that they are "unconvinced that there is a case yet made for pursuing significant further deepening of international co-ordination of banking regulation. Indeed, we believe it quite likely that greater exercise of national discretion is the appropriate path forwards."

Now I understand the conundrum that you cannot have one nation regulate for example to stop bank bonuses as it will just mean bankers jump across to other nations. So you need a global agreement of some form. Equally, no global agreement will work, as there is always gold-plating and protectionism of national instruments, so you need a global framework with local interpretation.

That is kinda what they've proposed, but it's rather unclear. For example, their closing comment on liquidity is:

"In our view, improving liquidity standards are amongst the most important and material changes to be introduced – though they are likely to have high costs that must be recognised. However, the scope for international standards to deliver adequate liquidity is limited without increased roles for national lenders of last resort and in particular an increased role for central banks in prudential supervision."

In fact, the regular mantra in the document appears to be the frictions and tensions between global and local. For example, they state that there is a "risk that regulation will not apply evenly or that regulation will apply in the UK before the rest of the world", and that this "is seen as a significant threat to London's competitiveness. It is therefore widely urged that the Basel measures enact a common international timetable. International firms that operate in multiple markets are particularly keen to see common, consistent frameworks and standards applied."

Yet, as mentioned, they don't think regulation will or can be applied consistently across multiple markets.

All in all, more questions raised than answers in this document, but worth a read for those who are technically minded and interested.

Will regulators destroy the banking system? (2010)

On April 1st, the European Commission announced their key work plans for 2010. The plans are wide-ranging and imply a fundamental restructuring of the European banking markets.

If you don't think it's going that far, then think again, as a wide range of strategic initiatives were announced, including a new European supervision architecture and proposals in areas covering everything from derivatives markets, short selling and credit default swaps, deposit guarantee schemes, market abuse, crisis management tools and bank capital requirements. On this last point, they are even mooting a bank levy to generate €50 billion in case of future bailouts.

Alongside all of this, you have the hoo-ha of Paul Volcker's proposals on getting rid of bank prop trading, which has now been shot down, and Gordon Brown's Tobin tax which may go by-the-by as a result of the UK general election.

Whichever way you look at it though, we have governments and regulators everywhere saying that things must change, and trying to work out how to change things.

Then you have all of the committees, such as the UK's Treasury Select Committee and the US congressionally chartered Financial Crisis Inquiry Commission, who are bank bashing on regular occasion to try to work out what things to change.

In the case of the latter, they've had regular visitations from bank leaders and other besmirched economists and thinkers, to find out what caused the financial car crash of 2008.

Of note in this parade of failed financial acolytes was the appearance of Alan Greenspan, the highly esteemed and now generally blamed former head of the US Federal Reserve. Mr. Greenspan makes regular appearances, blaming the crisis on everything from the fall of the Berlin Wall and China's emergence through globalisation, to the banks leveraging of subprime and complex trade-off and packaging of such debt through complex financial instruments.

In fact, about the only accurate thing he has said recently is that: "Regulators who are required to forecast have had a woeful record of chronic failure. History tells us they cannot identify the timing of a crisis, or anticipate exactly where it will be located or how large the losses and spillovers will be ... nor can they fully eliminate the possibility of future crises."

88

Now I don't want to make this a Greenspan bashing column, as that would be too easy, but I do want to pick up on that phrase: "a woeful record", as it is very relevant to where we are today.

For example, as the European Commission considers its wide-ranging changes, I could pick up on many of their previous attempts to regulate the markets that have yet to succeed and would beg the question: why don't you fix what you started whilst starting to work out what to fix?

After all, we have Basel III, UCITS IV, Solvency II and CRD IV all coming up. Notice something about those? Yes, they are all updates of earlier regulations that did not work as expected.

We have the same with regulations such as MiFID, the Markets in Financial Instruments Directive. In the 2010 workplan, the European Commission announced that they were going to be taking a review of MiFID to make legislative proposals that would include the "dark pools issue". What this demonstrates is the law of unintended consequences, where MiFID has made everything electronified, fragmented and opaque. The opposite of some of its intentions, which were for transparency and a level playing field.

In summary, what worries me right now is: first, that the regulators and policymakers are scrabbling around not knowing what to do; second, that they have obviously got it wrong in the past; third, that they are woeful at working at the future; and finally, that their whole focus on shaking up the banking system will destroy it.

Not being too much of a scaremonger, am I?

What happens if a country leaves the Eurozone? (2010)

It's a funny old world. One minute we're all talking about the great European plan, the Lisbon agenda, the Directives are rolled

*The Extraordinary Madness of Banks and the
Extreme Folly of Governments*

out, SEPA and MTFs are spawned, the level playing field of the Eurozone is harmonised and so on and so forth.

The next is OMG, it's all doom and gloom. What about Greece? Ireland? Portugal? Spain? Italy? This is a disaster!

Meanwhile, the Eurocrats continue to focus upon euro enlargement with Serbia, Macedonia, Montenegro, Albania and Bosnia all in the frame, as well as Turkey, of course. In fact, Turkey's chief negotiator on EU accession believes that: "the European Union needs Turkey more than Turkey needs the European Union". Very diplomatic ... and possibly true as Turkey represents the point where West meets East for many.

So what's the reality? I was thinking about this the other day, as someone asked me about Ireland's future.

To be honest, I don't think there's a problem if a country has to leave the European Union or the Eurozone. Think about it. So far, the reason why we balk at such an idea is because no-one's ever done it before. No country has left the European Union so far.

Some have changed and adapted, as in Germany is different today than 20 years ago thanks the Berlin Wall coming down. The UK is different to what it was 20 years ago, as we now have a Welsh and Scottish Assembly and a more stable Northern Ireland Assembly. Belgium is breaking apart into Franco-Belgique Wallonia and Dutch-Belgique Flanders. Yugoslavia exploded into the Serbian-Bosnian war, but it hasn't stopped Serbia and Bosnia seeking to join the Union.

So what of the future? Could Portugal leave the euro, as recently implied by their foreign minister, even though just nine months ago there was an emphatic view this could never happen. And what does it mean if a country leaves?

For the UK, it was a good thing. The UK left the Eurozone plan in 1992 thanks to George Soros and, ever since, we've thanked our lucky stars we did. UK sterling looks like a good bet in the short term against the euro, and we have been able to fully engage in actions to halt the slide into depression by printing money through the Quantitative Easing (QE) program and rapidly reducing interest rates to zero. All of the latter actions are impossible for Eurozone countries to engage in, as they are dependent on the policy across 16 countries controlled by the European Central Bank (ECB).

And there's the issue. The UK can issue bonds, t-bills, print money and create more debt because we are a strong country with strong investment yield and credit rating.

Portugal, Ireland, Greece and Spain don't have any of these capabilities.

First, they are not strong countries with good credit ratings, as demonstrated by the downgrade of Greece in April by Standard & Poors that kicked off this crisis of confidence.

Second, they cannot control any fiscal policy effectively as all interest rates are controlled by Frankfurt, which handcuffs these economies to centralised control.

Even more of an issue for these countries is that they cannot ease their debt burden by printing money through QE as the UK and USA have done. This is because it would have to be issued through the ECB again, and they have been loth to delve into such areas.

Even if Portugal, Ireland, Greece and Spain could print money, it would need to be substantiated by bonds and government treasury bills that had value to support such an increase in debt ... and these countries do not have the ability to sell such debt due to the downgrade of their credit status.

This is the real issue as Portugal, Ireland, Greece or Spain could leave the Eurozone and EMU ... but to go to what? If Ireland went back to the punt and Greece the drachma, what does this give them? It gives them the ability to control interest policies, print more money through QE and issue further debt ... but does anyone believe in or want such burdens from countries already teetering towards junk status? Maybe ... Argentina survived such a crisis, for example.

Others would say that, for the European Union, it's a good thing to get rid of basket case countries that weaken the Union. A small few might say that any country leaving the European Union or even the Eurozone is no issue. It may not have been done before, but that's no reason why it shouldn't happen and, if it did, it does not signal the end of the Union or the euro.

However, the bottom line is really that any country forced to leave the Eurozone would be an embarrassment to the Grand Plan. That's the main raison d'être for bailing out Greece and Ireland, and why Portugal would be bailed out too.

However, with over €1 trillion exposure in Spain, the big question is what happens if their economy tanks?

Mmmm ... we'll deal with that when it happens, I guess.

Europe's new regulatory agenda (2010)

We had a fascinating and packed meeting at the Financial Services Club this week with David Doyle, EU Policy Advisor, discussing the challenges of the new Barosso European Parliament and their legislative drive in financial services.

David is a regular visitor to the Financial Services Club, and runs our European Financial Regulatory Advisory Group.

In a broad and wide ranging speech, he presented key views around MiFID, the PSD, Solvency II, UCITS IV, Basel III and more, as well as commentary on Jacques de Larosière's committee and the appointment of Michel Barnier to succeed Charlie McCreevy.

Here's a summary of the key points David made.

The Commission is taking a 'safety first approach' to regulating capital markets and market actors, and will fill in the gaps where European or national regulation is insufficient or incomplete.

The over-riding principles of their approach are that:

◆   All that is of systemic importance should be regulated and supervised;

◆   There is a need for a better well-capitalised finance industry, with less leverage;

◆   The Commission must legislate to avoid the perverse incentives in the financial sector that encourage excessive risk taking or over-reward;

◆   Supervision should have the right tools to grasp complex, inter-connected and globalised financial activities; and

◆   To restore trust, investors and consumers should benefit from clearer, more coherent and effective safeguards.

At this point, audience members asked lots of questions about whether the European approach would be the same as, or co-ordinated with, the US approach. David's feeling is that it is being co-ordinated on the big ticket items – risk, leverage, capital, bonuses and such like – but the rest is still open competition in terms of the way payments, capital markets and specific aspects of the market are operating, such as hedge funds.

There are then the key changes that should be introduced by the new Barosso team in the near term as a result of the de Larosière report. Of these changes, David believes that the new supervisory bodies will be key here. These are:

◆   European Securities and Markets Authority (ESMA);

◆   European Banking Authority (EBA) ;

◆   European Insurance and Occupational Pensions Authority (EIOPA).

The Extraordinary Madness of Banks and the Extreme Folly of Governments

These new authorities will have teeth, and will be responsible for ensuring that any EU member states who are not following the line of regulatory oversight are brought to order.

This will be in play within two years:

◆ 2009–2010: National FSAs powers strengthened, plus a focus on harmonising national rules to reduce cross-border differences ;

◆ 2011–2012: Implement EU-wide supervision via ESMA/EBA/EIOPA which will mean that the large states which are proactively interpreting directives will be in a far stronger position than those states resisting such supervision;

In practice, this means the UK and the Netherlands are going to be fine; France and Germany will have some wrinkles to iron out; other nations will get a note to say they need to fine-tune some stuff; and Spain and Italy will get a large wet fish slapped around their chops. After all, every Directive I deal with – MiFID and the PSD in particular – it's Spain and Italy which always seem to be dragging their heels.

David also made an interesting point here, which is that not only will the new regulatory bodies have teeth to drag member states before Brussels to explain why they are dragging their heels, but also resources to assist when assistance is needed. Therefore, in the case of Sweden where their key person for transposition of the PSD left at a critical juncture, this future structure would allow the EBA – the European Banking Authority which is not to be confused with the EBA, the Euro Banking Association that operates STEP2 and EURO1 – to provide people to fill the gaps. These people may be promoted in from regulatory authorities in other EU member states for example and, in so doing, it will fill the gaps.

A happy medium for macroprudential supervision (2009)

In the dialogue of the past week or so, an interesting theme has emerged. The theme is globally harmonised rules.

In fact, there appears to be a tectonic plate shift towards some form of global neutrality. What I mean by this is that historically, the English have disliked the French and vice versa; the Americans have been wary of the Russians and vice versa; and the Chinese have not trusted most nations, and most nations have not trusted the Chinese. I get a sense that this is changing.

With the last world war between nations a half a century ago, when we realised the loss of life was too intolerable to bear, we have had a tense but workable trading relationship worldwide ever since. That trading relationship has been brought to a head over the past year though, as the credit crisis strained all cross-border trade and finance relationships.

America and China were rumoured to be starting trade wars; Russia clamped down on dissident bloggers and media reporting; Europe split into pro-banking and anti-banking blocks; and everyone has been on tenterhooks to see how the world and, more specifically, the G20, would work out these issues. And there's the rub: the G20 has to work out these issues and act in unison. Unilateral actions from one country, such as taxing bankers' bonuses, will just result in banks and bankers moving to other financial centres to avoid the unilateral actions.

(...)

We appear to be moving away from free markets and principles-based regulation to tightly controlled markets with Napoleonic law. The problem with the Napoleonic approach is that it means everything has to be written into the rules. That is because if it's not in the rules, then it is assumed to be permissible. Hence, you end up with rule upon rule, and bureaucracy upon bureaucracy.

So there has to be a happy medium between free market disciplines with self-regulation and tightly monitored markets with strong regulators.

All in all, what the G20 movement seems to be moving towards therefore is global macroprudential supervisory structures that will strike a balance between leveraged collateral coverage, entrepreneurialism and individual innovation with appropriate market checks and balances, and free markets structures with tightly coupled regulations.

Although some of these drivers, structures, rules and procedures appear to be at opposites with each other, what it really means is that the G20 has to navigate towards a globally agreed approach that works for all.

Tough call but, if they can do it, a worthwhile goal to strive for.

The biggest danger is that we end up with rules that operate based upon the lowest common denominator. This is what we have ended up with in Europe, where all Directives are agreed to cater for the least sophisticated member state at the expense of the sophistication of the most developed states.

Or that's what people are telling me in the banks, as they are forced to obsolete highly functional systems for ones that are less functional as a result of EU directives.

This game of macroprudential supervisory structures will be an interesting one to observe, and to discover whether we get the best or worst of all worlds ... or, most likely, something in between.

What's next for the EU in light of the financial crisis? (2009)

Eurofi had their annual conference in Gothenburg, Sweden last month. The meeting was themed 'What are the priorities for the incoming EU authorities in the light of the financial crisis' and saw a number of common themes recur in discussions by key policymakers, officials and industry figures.

Here is their summary of the meeting.

While it is clear that the worst of the crisis is behind us, we are not out of the woods yet.

This is in large part because one of the main underlying contributors to the crisis has not gone away: the existence of moral hazard. Indeed, it has probably got worse in the financial system because of the implicit acknowledgement that some institutions are too big or to interconnect to fail has in many cases become explicit.

This is an issue not just for the financial authorities but also for the single market. A total of €3 trillion has been injected into the EU's financial sector, but it has been distributed unevenly, creating potential distortions of the competitive landscape.

For this reason, as well as the massive burden placed on public finances, it is important to start thinking about an exit strategy that can extricate governments from some of Europe's largest financial groups.

However, the financial sector faces enormous issues of trust – the public has been appalled by what's happened. Many market participants have lost faith in each other, partly because the value of so many impaired assets remains so uncertain.

The debate continues over whether banks will be forced to narrow their activities, with influential figures such as Paul Volcker, economic adviser to President Obama, speaking out in favour of restrictions, while many in the industry argue that it was not business models that were to blame for the crisis but poor execution.

There is clear consensus that the crisis revealed unsuspected systemic risks and that these must be dealt with. Self-regulation has been thoroughly discredited and new regulation is on the way or has already been introduced in an attempt to harness the

The Extraordinary Madness of Banks and the
Extreme Folly of Governments

momentum for change that much fear is running out as the crisis recedes.

It is agreed that regulation and supervision of individual financial entities is not enough – there must be oversight of macro systemic risks as well, and this oversight must be linked to microprudential regulation, not just in the EU but on a global basis.

The industry is clearly unhappy at the weight of new regulation. Jacques de Larosière warns that there are dangers of unintended consequences from the overlapping of the various initiatives. Moreover, a system of ratios that would be to some extent disconnected from effective risks would do nothing to address the causes of this crisis. These measures will have a disproportionate impact on Europe where bank intermediation is far more developed than in the US.

However, policymakers have become more confident in their assertions that there are restrictions to the sector's freedom that are justified for the good of the system as a whole.

Nonetheless, it is recognised that significant challenges remain in implementing the regulation.

An unprecedented level of communication and co-operation will be necessary to ensure that overkill and regulatory arbitrage are avoided.

There must also be a re-examination of the financial system, of its role and size, some participants said. The world faces a range of significant, long-term challenges such as climate change, scarcity of natural resources and ageing population. Dealing with these requires a more long-term outlook from investors that has been lacking in recent years and to tackle obstacles long-term investment has to face up.

The regulatory framework of OTC derivatives and alternative investment funds (AIFs) is also being reviewed with the objective to bring additional safety to the financial system. The industry, however, points out that constraints that may be unnecessary from a risk mitigation perspective. Constraints potentially damaging to customer needs should be avoided, and the specificities of the products concerned should be well taken into account. The risk management processes of management companies should also be revised in light of the financial crisis and the responsibilities and liabilities of the players operating along the fund value chain should also be clarified.

Finally, the ongoing actions to improve the efficiency and competitiveness of cash equity infrastructures (MiFID and the Code of Conduct) should not create new risks particularly when implementing interoperability between CCPs.

As Jean-Claude Trichet, President of the European Central Bank, said: "While a lot has been achieved, a lot remains to be done."

Stress tests useful or misleading? (2010)

Having spent much of the weekend absorbing the European bank stress test results, I've got to ask why they bothered.

OK, so it was to get bank share prices up, but the whole thing was just a typical European sham where every country does things in a different way, with the whole thing designed to cover up the real weaknesses in the European banking system.

Bearing in mind that the stress tests were called to shore up confidence in the system due to the concerns in the markets over a sovereign default in Greece or Spain, the fact that the tests left out that particular scenario is ridiculous.

In case you didn't catch it, the tests looked at a double dip recession and a sovereign debt shock, but purely based upon debt that banks were trading, not debt that banks had in their vaults.

The Extraordinary Madness of Banks and the
Extreme Folly of Governments

Now I blogged a while back about the fact that Europe's banks held over $1 trillion in debt to just Greece and Spain.

With sovereign debt trading on the bank's books worth about a tenth of their total exposure, that means that around $900 billion of potential sovereign debt has been ignored. How this can be ignored is beyond me.

Secondly, the tests ignore any liquidity risk issues, and just looked at market and credit risks. Why?

This crisis started with liquidity risk when interbank lending dried up, and then exploded when sovereign debt became a major concern. The fact that CEBS left out these two clearly important dimensions just seems silly.

But then it is purely a politically motivated exercise to try to stop the haemorrhaging of confidence in the European system.

Now, I actually went to the press briefing on Friday night – a time chosen to ensure that markets could not react immediately to this sham – and saw the baying hounds of the media looking totally incredulous as the headlines were announced.

"We have seven bank failures that, between them, in the most adverse scenario would need €3.5 billion of new capital."

I'm sorry, but that's nuts.

When the Americans did their stress tests, half their banks failed and they needed $75 billion of new capital. So how come, in the worst of situations, our banks would only need €3.5 billion and fewer than 10% fail?

Because it's a fix. It's fixed because each country interpreted the stress test conditions for unemployment and house prices and other economic conditions in their own way.

It's fixed because each regulator and central bank applied the test conditions against their bank's balance sheets in different ways.

And it's fixed by leaving out the sovereign debt exposures and potential defaults on the bank's books.

Nevertheless, something useful did come out of it: data. There's lots of data about the state of the bank's balance sheets released by CEBS that can now be analysed by the markets, rather than the fudge that the regulators applied. Therefore, with the reservations stated above, I went through the numbers over the weekend and found an interesting result.

First, a little explanation of the numbers.

The tests are based upon three scenarios.

Scenario 1 is the benchmark, which is based upon the current ECB forecasts for macroeconomic developments across the European Union.

Scenario 2 is then based upon a double dip recession, which sees no growth in 2010 and a 0.4% downturn in GDP in the European Union in 2011, versus 1% in 2010 and 1.7% forecasted in the benchmark.

Scenario 3 studies the impact of a sovereign debt shock to the European Union on top of this recession, and is geared towards higher debt losses and impairments in the PIIGS – Portugal, Ireland, Italy, Greece and Spain – than in other countries.

This does not assume a sovereign default, just corporate debt and sovereign debt on the trading books of the banks. That's about 10% of the total exposure for the banks, should a country default.

In the CEBS tests, they looked at Tier 1 capital ratio – not core capital, just Tier 1 capital – and said that the ratio should not fall under 6%. Under the EU Capital Requirements Directive, as it stands uncorrected since this crisis hit, the lowest level by law is 4%. Meanwhile, the likelihood is that a minimum 8% Tier 1 capital will be required in the future and, in this context, is a far better ratio to apply.

For example, based upon the CEBS view of the world, using the combined worst case of a double dip recession and a sovereign debt shock, they find seven banks would fall under the 6%

Tier 1 capital ratio level: five in Spain, one in Germany and one in Greece.

Looking at the numbers using an 8% Tier 1 capital levels – a level that is rumoured to be required under revised terms for EU bank trading in the future – 39 banks would fail in the worst-case scenario: one in Austria, one in Cyprus, five in Germany, three in Greece, two in Ireland, four in Italy, one in Portugal, one in Slovenia and 21 in Spain.

That would have been a far more realistic number to have announced and, based upon the fragmented application and interpretation of the tests by member states, is probably more likely to be the worst-case scenario than the seven bank failures CEBS announced last Friday.

Note: Failure does not means the banks are insolvent just undercapitalised, and so this would have been a much better way for CEBS, the ECB and the European Commission to have achieved some credibility from this exercise.

Stressed? Don't worry. The French and Germans will sort it out … (2010)

The reason CEBS, the European Commission and European Central Bank gave for not including the scenario of a sovereign default in the stress tests is that they just don't think it's going to happen.

"It is not possible", they said. "Why", we asked. "Because it is just incredibly unlikely and, even if anything did start to fragment in the fissures of finance in Greece or Spain, we have the European Financial Stability Fund (EFSF) to solve it", they replied.

Now that's an interesting statement … because it is also a fuddle. The EFSF is a €440 billion fund designed to cover any sovereign debt crisis in Europe in the future. Therefore, the concept of a bank being exposed to huge losses from Greece and Spain is no longer an issue. That is the logic. And it's quite good. But it's already been shot to pieces.

Ken Wattret, a market analyst with BNP Paribas, performed a really interesting analysis of the EFSF and issued a note in July that provides a clear Q&A overview. Here's my summary of Ken's research note:

> The EFSF is a limited liability company based in Luxembourg announced in May as a measure to "preserve financial stability in Europe". Its CEO is Klaus Regling, a former senior German Finance Ministry official who worked on the preparations for EMU and who has also worked at the IMF.
>
> The purpose of the EFSF, according to its terms of reference, is "to collect funds and provide loans in conjunction with the IMF to cover the financing needs of Eurozone member states in difficulty, subject to strict conditionality".
>
> According to the Framework Agreement, the EFSF will finance the provision of loans via the issuance of "bonds, notes, commercial paper, debt securities or other financing arrangements" which will be backed by unconditional and irrevocable guarantees from those member states which participate.
>
> Only the member states of the Eurozone participate in the scheme, providing guarantees up to a total of €440bn on a pro-rata basis.
>
> If a Eurozone member state seeks assistance from the EFSF, they must initially agree a Memorandum of Understanding (MoU) with the European Commission, in liaison with the IMF and the ECB. This MoU will set out the budgetary and economic policy conditions which the Eurozone

member state must comply with in order to receive financial assistance.

The detailed terms and conditions would then be set out in a Loan Facility Agreement which is subject to the agreement of all the guarantors (i.e. those countries in the EFSF).

The EFSF will enter into force when five or more member states, comprising at least two-thirds of the total guarantees, have confirmed that they have concluded the necessary procedures under their national legislation. It will last for almost three years, with the guarantees applying to loans made on or before 30 June 2013.

Now then, what Mr. Wattret did next is the most intriguing part. He produced a chart which shows that Germany and France contribute almost half of all of the ECB's capital for this scheme, whilst the PIIGS – Portugal, Italy, Ireland, Greece and Spain – contribute almost 35% of the scheme, with Italy and Spain representing 30%. Greece does not contribute anything to the scheme at this time for obvious reasons.

So what the ECB is saying is that the $1 trillion exposure of European banks to the sovereign debt of just Greece and Spain, as discussed yesterday, can be covered by the €440 billion available in an emergency through this scheme.

But let's take this a step further. Say Spain gets into distress and has to leave the scheme. That removes a further 12% of the scheme's funding. In fact, should Spain have issues, the burden on France and Germany increases by a further 7% of the fund – or an additional €7.5 billion to bring their number to a total of €250 billion between them.

This is what prompted me to ask at the end of the CEBS press conference: "So what you're really saying is that you didn't use the scenario of a sovereign default because you believe French and

German citizens will be happy to bail out Spain like they did with Greece?"

That didn't go down well but it had to be asked and, no matter how unlikely it is for this to occur, it is the reality of the situation.

Chapter 4 Banks' inaction?

Introduction

Whilst politicians and regulators run around trying to create new rules and policies, banks have also been active. Their actions were primarily directed at ensuring the new procedures and regulations would continue to work to their advantage, rather than tightening the noose so much that innovations in banking activities would become impossible. Whilst the policymakers were trying hard to return banks to their roots of lending when appropriate and investing where necessary, banks were trying hard to ensure that the high wave of profits made available through innovative investment markets would continue. The result has been a tension between willingness to change and support an agenda to avoid future crisis and a need to maintain the status quo to ensure that profitability and arbitrage could still be played as before. Some view this as banks' inaction, whilst others view it as the fine line between winners and losers. You make your own mind up.

Playing ping-pong with bank's yachts (2011)

After my note the other day about the thoughts of folks in transaction banking, followed by the results of the US banks that shows a big slowdown in equities, fixed income and commodity trading, it struck me that like a double-dip recession we are now in a ping-pong interregnum.

What do I mean? During a period of long-term stability, like the early to mid 2000s, where results were relatively predictable, markets were resilient, conditions were benign and the headwinds favourable, all the banks invested in innovation programs for growth.

Then we hit the turbo turbulence of the Global Financial Crisis and everything went bananas. Nothing was certain, everyone was panicking, markets were tumbling, and everything was going south, all the banks invested in cost cutting and risk management.

By the end of 2010, things seemed to have come back to some kind of norm and so the talk of growth and investment was back on the agenda. Now it's going off the agenda again, as headcounts are being shed and cost cutting is back.

In other words, the uncertainty of markets is causing many banks to have strategies that are about as robust as a yacht with a sail full of holes. The yacht's going nowhere, regardless of the wind's direction. Last quarter, it's growth and innovation. This quarter, it's cost cutting and risk. Next quarter it's growth and risk. The quarter after that, it's innovation through cost-cutting.

Who knows what strategy some banks are following, as it's just completely tactical and reactive. The thing is that you cannot have a wholly reactive strategy. A wholly reactive strategy is a strategy shot through of holes.

So what do banks need to do in these turbulent times? Well, they need to have a strategy for a start. The strategy has to be where they want to get to in the next few years. We could talk missions and visions, objectives and key performance indicators but, more importantly, we need to talk about a direction. A place the bank wants to be.

At least if a bank has that direction, then they can change the yacht's course to suit either wind: the strong headwind that wants them to turn or the supportive tailwind that sets them on their way.

After all, with a direction, at least the bank can turn from the headwinds but still know what course they are going to charter, rather than these ping-pong strategies that just say speed on, turn back, speed on, turn back.

Guess what? That gets you nowhere.

Psychos, maniacs and nutters: the average trading room (2011)

An aspect of trading that cropped up last week was the whole thing about trading psychologies. This was kicked off by one of the speakers, a psychology professor, exploring the psychology of trading. In his and many other studies, trading is very much akin to madness, with 'the deal' being linked to gambling, sex and worse.

One of the best examples of such madness is described in the book and movie 'American Psycho' by Bret Easton Ellis, about a guy who is a Wall Street trader by day and a homicidal maniac by night:

> "I have all the characteristics of a human being: blood, flesh, skin, hair; but not a single, clear, identifiable emotion, except for greed and disgust. Something horrible is happening inside of me and I don't know why. My nightly bloodlust has overflown into my days. I feel lethal, on the verge of frenzy. I think my mask of sanity is about to slip."

A fine line between sanity and madness in the trading rooms of the world's financial markets. If you don't think so, then check-out another fine book by David Charters, a former investment banker: 'At Bonus Time, No-one Can Hear You Scream' (free eBook, courtesy of efinancial news):

"Last night I killed my boss. It was the second time this week, only this time it was much worse. He was sitting at his desk in his big, glass-sided, corner office, looking out at the trading floor with its hundreds of identical workstations, the computer screens, the phones, and us, the worker bees who feed the machine. Looking at us, as we stayed late in the run-up to the annual bonus round, putting in face time to look good, keeping busy, trying to persuade him how essential we all were. Well, I'd had enough."

The truth is the markets are mad, and the people who work the markets are mad. If you want any more proof, then just check out the true story of the 'Wolf of Wall Street', Jordan Belfort.

As a 31-year-old multimillionaire stockbroker, Belfort once landed his helicopter on his back lawn, flying with just one eye open because he was so stoned he had double vision. He sank his 167ft motor yacht, complete with seaplane and helicopter, after overruling the captain and taking it into a Mediterranean storm. He organised a midget-throwing contest to entertain brokers on his trading floor. And when he wasn't completely out of his head on drugs, or getting executive relief from prostitutes in the presidential suites of luxury hotels, the man nicknamed the Wolf of Wall Street was presiding over a firm that swindled investors out of $200 million in a shares fraud that landed him and his chief confederates in prison.

I could name many more illustrations – both factual and fiction – of the madness of markets, but the core of how to work these markets is to detach the madness from the rational. To be detached and remote from the action, and to watch it with a heart rate of 80bpm or less. After all, going back to our psychology professor's presentation, he makes clear that it is emotions that ruin traders.

Citing experiments by various psychologists just shows that all sorts of factors from sunshine and clouds to wind and the cycles of the moon affect our trading strategies.

Take this one: 'Affective Influence on Judgments and Decisions: Moving Towards Core Mechanisms', by Piotr Winkielman, Martin Paulus and Jennifer L. Trujillo of the University of California, with Brian Knutson of Stanford University. In this 2007 experiment, people were shown angry and happy faces and tested to see how it affected their decision-making. Interestingly, those who had seen the angry and frightened faces were far more risk-averse than those who saw the happy ones.

111

This explains the madness of crowds. If everyone's happy, you follow the crowd; if everyone's sad, you are too. It's all about the pre-frontal cortex and what makes us man, and is the reason why Warren Buffett says: "Be fearful when others are greedy, and be greedy when others are fearful".

Do bankers really want to be plumbers? (2010)

I was preparing a presentation last week that had the sexy title: "Challenges for European banks in a crisis and post-crisis environment." It wasn't a title I chose, but led to me creating an amalgam of many different threads of thinking.

First, I thought about all the things that we refer to today as phrases which mean something, and yet weren't even around three or four years ago. These phrases include:

◆ Credit crunch;
◆ Sub-prime crisis;
◆ High frequency trading;
◆ Flash crash
◆ Banksters.

My own personal favourite is the 'Vampire Squid 'that is Goldman Sachs. These are now in the public psyche and are used regularly in conversation, along with other more complex terms like Structured Investment Vehicles, Credit Default Swaps and Mortgage-Backed Securities.

I then thought about the things that policymakers are talking about in response to the above. These include:

◆ Austerity measures;
◆ Quantitative easing;
◆ Basel III;
◆ Liquidity risk;
◆ Capital ratios;

112

◆   OTC derivatives.

On Basel III in particular, the landscape is confused. This was hotly debated at SIBOS for example, with Standard Chartered stating that the new regulations would lead to trade finance becoming 15% to 37% more expensive, with volumes reducing by 6% – equivalent to a $270 billion a year reduction in global trade – and a 0.5% fall in global GDP.

Werner Steinmuller, who leads the transaction banking services for Deutsche Bank, agreed at the Frankfurt Euro Finance meeting I attended last week, saying that, due to trade finance issues, global trade will go down 6%, resulting in a 20% increase in pricing for instruments and a 0.3% fall in global GDP.

Interestingly the International Chamber of Commerce published a study looking at the default risk of trade finance instruments, and finds that the regulations are potentially punishing trade. The study examined the trade finance activity of nine global banks from 2005 to 2009, which together arranged 5.2 million transactions accounting for $2.5 trillion. It found that only 1,140 of those transactions defaulted. Of the 2.8 million transactions arranged during the crisis in 2008 and 2009, only 445 defaulted.

Percentage wise that's a 0.016% default rate. In olden parlance, that's diddly-squat, and it makes you wonder whether the regulators are using a sledgehammer to bang in a very small nail. After all, they are doing the same with OTC derivatives and other regulatory areas, and cannot even agree common definitions for half of this stuff, so regulations are a big of a confused mess.

Which brings me to the final area of background: the big issues. The big issues remain the same: bank governance and behaviours. Here we have phrases like:
◆   Moral compass;
◆   Ethics;
◆   Bonuses;
◆   Lending,

The Extraordinary Madness of Banks and the Extreme Folly of Governments

and other things in the fray. In this area, the regulators and policy-makers have little clue what to do as if they act on their own, they are likely to alienate the industry and find a huge loss of tax revenues if, as would be anticipated, the banks and their employees relocated. But waiting to act as a cohesive G20 whole is also just as unlikely, so these things will remain the same.

Nevertheless, I do think there will be a rethinking of the bank code of conduct, with the leadership of the industry taking a stand to try to improve the image. In the UK, this has certainly been the case under BBA Chairman Stephen Green, who has created a lending taskforce during the Autumn, and I fully expect such coordinated response to be created for other areas, although bonuses doesn't seem to be one of them.

The most important area, however, is the customer. Not just the retail customer, the Gen "Y am I broke" customer or the business customer. All customers.

Customers will demand a revolution of banking, and some already are. But the real revolution will come about due to the fact that this planet has now connected every individual, so that they don't need institutions. The ability to create new currencies through social P2P services is potentially very disruptive. Except that the pipework and plumbing of payments will remain where it's always been: with the banks. And that's the real question in this post-crisis, zero trust world of finance: can banks be anything more than just plumbing in tomorrow's world?

Rethinking the customer experience (2010)

Just got a really interesting survey from Deloitte looking at the future of financial services. The document is based upon a survey of 200 industry execs, and garners their views across a broad brush of areas.

Interestingly, 89% of those surveyed believe their firm survived the crisis as expected or better than expected. I expect you can guess who's in the 11% who thought their firm suffered badly. Now most of them are looking at recovery and 88% are positive about the future ... I expect you can guess who's in the 12% who aren't.

Anyways, there are loads of question in there, but here's a few charts that really intrigued me.

In answer to the question: 'What strategic objectives of your business do you think have experienced the most long-term damage from the financial crisis and economic downturn?' more bankers than securities folks were worried about their ability to continue operating as they did in the past.

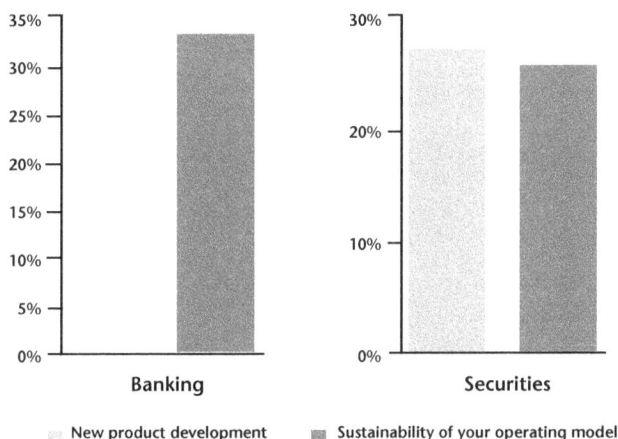

New product development   Sustainability of your operating model

In fact, it amazes me that 66% of bankers and 75% of securities personnel are therefore answering this question as 'business as usual'. What planet are they on?

Similarly, when asked 'what positive opportunities have resulted from the financial crisis and economic downturn?', the answer is overwhelmingly that competitors have been squeezed out of the market but, more intriguingly, Europeans are far more focused upon cost reductions than the Americans.

Now, I keep hearing that this crisis was caused by US investment banks ... so how come it's Europe that's cutting the costs?

And what are they going to do strategically about it? Well, most are going to focus upon better measurement of risks.

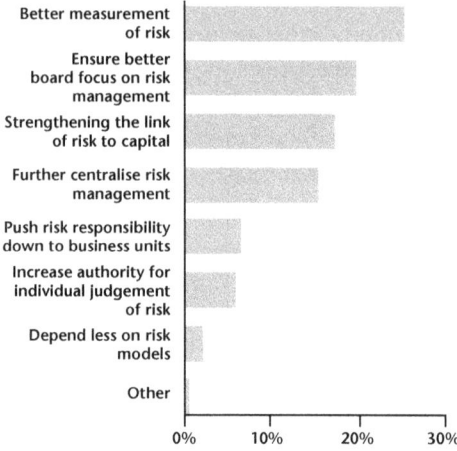

No wonder we all hear stuff about liquidity risk and real-time risk management these days.

Finally, most of the banks agree that it is customers and their relationship with customers that has been hit hardest by this crisis. Therefore their #1 focus is to rebuild relationships. How will they do that? By focusing upon improving the customer experience.

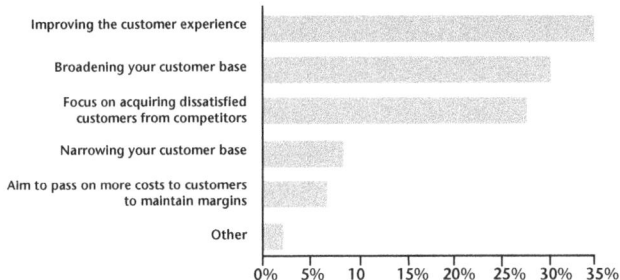

Improving the customer experience
Broadening your customer base
Focus on acquiring dissatisfied customers from competitors
Narrowing your customer base
Aim to pass on more costs to customers to maintain margins
Other

0%   5%   10   15%   20%   25%   30%   35%

Now then, who's doing that? What examples are out there of customer experience improvements? Aha, I know one. Checkout BBVA's ATM of the Future.

Fascinating stuff.

The land of a thousand voices (2010)

It seems that I'm having a long whinge and rant all week, but I'm trying not to.

What I'm really trying to do is to get some answers to this crisis of confidence in the banks and, consequently, the banking system. This is nothing to do with the credit crisis, but the response of the banks to the credit crisis, which is to trash all trust and confidence in their ethics and approach.

This is why there is this non-stop bleating about bonuses and interest rates. The banks justify this behaviour on the basis of all the other kids on the block are doing it so, if we didn't, we would just get beaten up in the banking playground by the bonus bullies. Stephen Hester of RBS said today that: "employees are leaving because it was offering lower bonuses than City rivals". He also said that profits at the bank, which is 84 per cent owned by the taxpayer, would have been about £1 billion higher if it had managed to stop staff leaving. The bank said it had "paid the minimum necessary to retain and motivate staff who are critical to the recovery of RBS".

Trouble is, this doesn't cut the mustard. MPs warned that the public would be astonished that the bank was paying £1.3 billion in bonuses, given that it today reported a £3.6 billion loss for last year.

But none of these arguments raging in the media address the real issue here. The real issue is not bonuses, profits, lending or interest rates. The real issue is a lack of internal market leadership within the banking industry.

Nothing to do with regulators, politicians or press. The most significant failure has been the inability for the industry to act as a cohesive whole to respond to the issues arising under their watch.

Instead we act as a fragmented group of a thousand voices. Individual voices stand up and are counted, and some count more than others such as the Jamie Dimons, John Varleys and Stephen Greens. But nothing is co-ordinated or arranged in a way that makes sense or alleviates the public anger and distrust in the system.

Take the example of the past week of bankers' bonuses. Initially, one bank – Barclays – set an example of waiving bonuses payments, as their leaders chose to repeat the actions of a year earlier and declined the multimillion pound pot they were entitled to. Reluctantly, the rest then followed with RBS, Lloyds and now HSBC one-by-one agreeing not to award their leader's bonus.

The result is that they were accused of being lame sheep in doing so, just following the lead of one, and it just looked limp. It also rang of insincerity anyway, in that several of these leaders are purely deferring bonuses and have taken large swags of cash via other means (e.g. Bob Diamond's $46 million payout on the sale of Barclays Global Investors last year) or just don't need it as most are on million-pound plus packages. In fact, one cynic said that there would just be a top-up of their pension pots to compensate,

118

and so no-one sees these token gestures as being anything other than that – token.

Does this justify the payouts to their investment banking teams by making such sacrifices? No. Does it restore faith and trust and displace the anger and mistrust?

No. So all it's done is served as some form of internal justification for the continuance of mega-bonus payments to investment banking staff.

The issue still lies with the press, politicians and regulators, however: in this land of 1,000 voices, where no one co-ordinated single voice resonates, where is the leadership to change the system?

Take the example I've just given. What bankers should have done is worked together to create a co-ordinated plan across the sector pre-emptively and early on. For example, Stephen Hester (RBS), John Varley and Bob Diamond (Barclays), Eric Daniels (Lloyds) and Michael Geoghegan (HSBC) see each other often enough in front of Treasury Select Committees to be able to co-ordinate their responses. So why didn't they all agree upfront to defer leaders' bonus payments, and announce this as a co-ordinated approach pre-results season? A joint announcement of rationale and reasoning would have been far more powerful than the sheep mentality manner of following the leader.

Equally, Jamie 'Demon' Dimon (JPMC), Vikram Pandit (Citi), Lloyd Blankfein (Goldman Sachs), Brian Moynihan (Bank of America) and John Mack (Morgan Stanley) see each other all the time in front of Federal Committees. So why didn't these leaders co-ordinate responses to bailouts and bonuses?

You may say they did, but not from an observer's viewpoint externally. It looks like maverick individual actions and approaches, with no single voice to rally the industry to a resolution.

Why these 'leaders' cannot organise themselves is beyond comprehension. After all, if these global CEOs of banks had created a co-ordinated and rational campaign to cap bonuses, waive their own, provide charitable donations, show how bank lending and bailouts had been atoned, then the media, public and politicians would not be baying for their blood.

The fact that: (a) there is no single voice of leadership that is co-ordinated across these banks speaking on their behalf; and (b) these leaders have allowed banks to behave without change, as they were before and as if nothing had happened, is going to lead to a showdown.

That showdown is not far away and, according got all my sources, will be far more draconian and vicious than any action that would have been taken if the industry had spoken with one voice, rather than a thousand.

But then, this industry's ability to self-regulate with transparency and integrity historically has been pretty poor so this comes as little surprise.

Banking on the banking system, one year later (2009)

At a recent event, the plenary session was all about 'leading through uncertainty' with:

◆ Peter Sands, Group Chief Executive of Standard Chartered;

◆ Ronnie Chan, Chairman of Hang Lung Properties Ltd; and

◆ Bill White, Chair of the OECD Economic and Development Review Committee,

discussing the state of the banking industry one year after its near-destruction and chaired by Martin Wolf, Chief Economics Commentator for the *Financial Times*.

Here's my summary of how their conversation went:

Martin Wolf: Is the financial system healed?

Peter Sands: 'Healed' is too strong a word. Better yes, but healed is too strong. For me, think of the patient as dying and now we've moved out of the operating theatre and intensive care, but that doesn't mean the financial system has left the hospital.

We still have huge imbalances which are an issue for the world economy and financial system and we still need to take leverage out of the system which has begun, but not happened to anywhere near the level it needs to yet.

Governments and central banks have thrown huge amounts of money at the system as well, but without an exit strategy.

Then there are a whole slew of things for the regulatory architecture to fix and, finally, there's a lot that we as banks need to mend as the business models of some of the banks are just not sustainable. For example, one of the biggest banking models until this time last year was the US broker-dealer model. Within a week of Lehman Brothers collapsing, that model ceased to exist, and the ramifications of that demise are still to filter through in terms of the wholesale lending markets.

At present, those markets have the support of the funding from central banks but, when that goes, then there will be further questions. For example, the cost of credit will go up and policymakers seem to think that banks and their shareholders will accept lower levels of return on credit but that is just not the case. The capital equation is therefore a difficult one.

Equally, the banker sector is more consolidated and concentrated now than it was before the crisis, so the idea of more competition rather than less as a result of these issues is also incorrect.

Ronnie Chan: If the question is whether the financial systems is healed or not, I think we have not even gone to see the doctor yet. Many of the issues are not even addressed. Let's face it, the

*The Extraordinary Madness of Banks and the
Extreme Folly of Governments*

Western financial system is far better than the Asian, but it is not a perfect systems and we need to address the issues we face.

I still think that commercial banking and investment banking should not mix for example. They do not belong in the same house and yet no-one is talking about Glass-Steagall and bringing it back. We need to do that as we need to define these parameters in the banks. Unless we define between and separate these sorts of banks, we still have issues.

Some people are even talking about shadow banking coming back already, and I fear that unless commercial and investment banking are put into a clearer perspective we will have all these issues again.

There's a problem with regulation as well, both under- and over-regulation depending upon where you look. By definition, regulation will always be behind product design and that is something we need to address, as many do not know of risks until after they occur.

On the final area, about the argument that we have to pay good bonuses to get the best brains, I would argue that if, by eliminating bonuses we lose those brains, then hallelujah.

Bill White: There's a question about a return to normalcy and getting back to equilibrium, but we haven't talked about rolling back all that leverage yet, all those CDOs, ABSs, MBOs, SIVs etc, so we're not out of the woods yet. We also worried about banks being too big and too complex to fail and yet now, two years into this crisis, the banks are even bigger and more complicated than ever before and every big bank is a universal bank mixing investment and commercial banking.

My concern is that these big banks will turn out to be zombie banks, and that they are too impaired to get the economic fuel moving again. Another concern is that they'll now get even more cavalier than they were before the crisis, and credit lending standards will deteriorate further as a consequence.

Mervyn King said that if a bank is too big to fail then it's not a viable bank, and that's where we need to focus for the future of regulation. In fact, I agree with Lord Turner of the FSA's view that we need every bank to create a 'living will'. Institutions must have plans to close themselves down lodged with the regulators, and if they cannot show that plan to the regulator then they must unbundle themselves from their complexity until they can, as Lord Turner has proposed.

Peter Sands: There's much here that I agree with but where I do not is if we go for any form of new Glass-Steagall lite. That is just a distraction. It wouldn't work. Supposedly we can have narrow banks that can go bust and that's alright. This would be the Bear Stearns, Washington Mutual, Northern Rock. What you actually get through Glass-Steagall in this case, however, is regulatory arbitrage which was a key contributor to the crisis. Therefore I think we need to regulate institutions regardless of what business they're in rather than trying to narrow their business.

The idea of a living will is also flawed in that, if you only rely upon regulation to restrain entrepreneurial exuberance, you will undoubtedly get another crisis. You need market discipline too. So we should be looking for who is too big to fail, what would happen if they did and a market discipline to manage that uncertainty.

I also don't like the phrase 'living will'. A will is meant to be the spreading of your assets that you distribute to your heirs whereas, for a bank, it is the opposite. How do you distribute your problems to others if you fail?

Martin Wolf: What about future growth then?

Peter Sands: Markets are thrilled that we're not disappearing over a cliff but no-one knows where we are going next. The view used to be that the world had this model where Asia produced and the West consumed but that model has gone. So where is the growth of demand going to come from? That is a structural issue and will be a reflection of domestic demand and balances across the emerging economies to rectify rather than the West, and that will take time. So there is a risk that this recovery will slow or stutter.

Bill White: We have very, very deep-seated problems here that could have led to bad deflation as in debt deflation. Well, the authorities stepping in and using Keynesian methods stopped all that. But what have been the side effects? What are the long-term implications of those responses to deflation? I worry about that. In fact, I worry about three specific things.

First, inflation. This is not a long-term thing as the issues are deflationary today but with quantitative easing, deflationary issues may come unstuck at some point. We've seen this in Latin America and over many decades perceptions of changes in the monetary regime can have a big impact on the economy. It will be very hard to know how to tighten things when needed. So I worry about deflation short-term and inflation long-term.

The second thing I worry about is asset prices. Yet again we are trying to get out of things the way we did last time, by generating another asset bubble. I worry about that.

Lastly, I worry about what many of the governments are doing is getting in the way of the structural adjustments that are required to correct the economy. We have industries that are too big – the auto industry, construction industry, banking industry – along with geographical imbalances between importers and exporters. Then the UK and USA does this 'cash for clunkers' deal and I take the view that the car industry is too big and what do we do? We create false demand and incentives to buy more cars to make the industry even bigger, which got us into the issue before: an industry that is too big.

So I'm worried about everything.

Peter Sands: I think a lot of this crystallises about what happens with the dollar and we can see a very volatile future for the dollar.

124

China has an exquisitely balanced equation between wanting to see the dollar play a less dominant role as the reserve currency, but then they also have a lot of dollars and don't want to lose the value of that investment.

Ronnie Chan: China cannot save the world as it's not big enough – China has a $4tn GDP versus $40tn amongst the largest group of seven others,

True, they pumped $200bn into the economy every month for several months, but what sectors are they stimulating? Infrastructure, and that is government-led. That is the sector doing its job.

You are not dealing with an economy that is purely market driven either, but one that is still centrally led. So they can drive change.

You don't change 3,000 years of frugality being a virtue as a culture in a few months.

Peter Sands: I think there have been some positive developments in regulation in terms of the Financial Stability Board, the dialogue globally, the acceptance of a need to be coordinated and consistent in reponse. This is a significant step forward. As an industry we do need better regulation as good banks get damaged by bad regulations.

There is a danger that we maybe get too focused upon this particular crisis and the closing of the stable doors for just these issues, which creates another set of issues downstream. I think we are doing this in some ways.

Equally, we are potentially creating an industry of overly complex and opaque regulation, by having too many cooks spoil the broth in terms of risk managers, compliance officers, accountants and auditors all in there trying to add to the equation. We also maybe get too embroiled in all the risks of liquidity and credit, and lose sight of what it is we are here to do as banks. There were issues in this area in Basel II for example, and there is a danger of more of this happening now.

There's too much focus upon the institutional structures of regulation as well, such as the UK's debate about who has control: the FSA, the Bank of England or the Treasury. The debate should be more about what regulators can do and should do well. Many of the failures of regulation were not because they couldn't do something but because they failed to execute their duties properly. That is not to excuse the bankers, but if we don't have the right rules, well executed and to work against, then we don't have a clear path forward.

Bill White: There's a lot of people focusing upon what was new that went wrong and say that if we could just fix all of that then all will be good. There is one camp, for example, who just want to tackle SIVs and CDOs and just fix that. But we should focus upon what was the same that caused this and other crises. The underlying issues that led to previous collapses. We are going to address these by taking the systemic issues and placing them front and centre this time.

Chapter 5 Too big to fail?

Introduction

One of the major refrains of the Global Financial Crisis, or GFC as some refer to it, has been the discussion of whether banks can be too big to fail, or TBTF, as others refer to it. The too big to fail debate has been particularly apropos, as the whole financial crisis has been predicated upon the issues of a global interconnectivity between a very small number of banks. These banks and their worldwide influence has led to politicians and regulators considering whether to limit a bank's scale in the future and potentially to break up the banks that are over-sized today. The danger of such action is that it could potentially damage already weakened economies, as well as dramatically altering the ability for banks to compete in the future. This dilemma is one that cannot be resolved easily, with the most common suggestion being that banks can operate globally at major size and scale, but they must do so with a 'living will' that details how they would untangle the web they have woven should they ever be in a position of failure. This is not ideal, but at least some sort of compromise is better than nothing.

Let the bank tax and accounting wars begin (2011)

After the bank reporting season in the UK last week, the most notable row that has emerged – alongside bonuses and a lack of lending – is the lack of taxes banks pay.

Banks are remarkably adept at being tax efficient – or should we say, tax avoiders – and this has been known for years. It is tolerated by governments as the taxes they avoid are all legitimate accounting techniques to minimise corporation tax whilst, on the other hand, they are big payers of national insurance contributions, pay-as-you-earn and other employee earnings-related taxes.

This conundrum puts governments in a bind: if they clamp down too hard on their banks, then they lose a possibly major chunk of tax revenues. However, by not clamping down on the banks, they lose a major chunk of tax revenues anyway.

This dilemma is the one facing the UK government in particular, as they see a dysfunctional banking system that they want to tax heavily but they know that, if they do, the banks will leave.

This was clearly demonstrated by the often mooted rumour about HSBC relocating to Hong Kong – that's been around since Michael Geoghegan's office moved there two years ago, although it's interesting that new CEO Stuart Gulliver has clearly said the office should be in London – and Barclays to New York.

Such sabre-rattling frightens the likes of George Osborne and Vince Cable, but does it frighten the likes of Mervyn King and Sir John Vickers? Probably not, as Mervyn King has been quite outspoken about bankers' bonuses and poor treatment of customers whilst promoting the idea that banks should be split between boring banking – retail and commercial – and casino banking – investments. A view that appears to be increasingly endorsed by Sir John Vickers, who will provide the regulatory framework for long-term bank reform later this year.

If it does go this way – higher taxes on bonuses and salaries, the forced split of proprietary trading (the casino bit of investment banking) and general restructuring, then be assured that it will mean the banks will relocate. Not Lloyds and RBS – the government-owned banks – but the big two of the big four: HSBC and Barclays.

Now, is this a big loss? Yes and no. It comes back to the taxation piece. According to a report by Pricewaterhouse Coopers, banks more than pay their way in the UK economy. The industry contributed an estimated £53.4 billion to UK government taxes in the 2009/10 financial year, accounting for 11.2% of the total UK tax take.

The figure, which excludes the 50% top rate of tax and the Bank Payroll Tax, is down by £8 billion from the previous fiscal year, but the sector has overtaken North Sea oil and gas to become once again the largest payer of corporation tax in 2010. The sector employs over one million workers which helped to generate £24.5 billion in employment taxes.

Wonderful. That's slightly less than the amount stated by the banks in Project Merlin's documentation, where the banks say they will "contribute a cumulative £8 billion of total tax take (covering direct and indirect sources, including the Bank Levy and VAT) in 2010 and, on the same basis, £10 billion in 2011."

But what's £45 billion here or there? The real issue is that the banks can easily offset tax liabilities based upon clever accounting. For example, leading accountant Richard Murphy writes that the UK banks received an effective subsidy of £19 billion, by writing down this amount as deferred tax liabilities due to expected losses in 2008:

"If some £19 billion in tax might not be paid as a result at some time in the future, there is an extraordinary double subsidy going on for these banks. Not only were their losses underwritten by the state in 2008 (and in most cases they still are receiving some form of state support, if only by way of asset guarantees), but they will now receive a second round of subsidy when over years to come they will offset those state subsidised losses against the profits they might now make only because they have been saved for the benefit of their shareholders by the UK government."

So there is some issue here about tax isn't there? It's one raised often by the Treasury Select Committee and, in particular, by campaigner MP Chuka Umunna who asked Bob Diamond how many offshore companies the bank had in global tax havens.

About 300, Bob Diamond answered. No wonder they only managed to pay £113 million in corporation tax last year. That was on the back of pre-tax profits in of £11.6 billion.

130

Similar questions are being raised by analysts about Lloyds and HSBC.

For example, Lloyds Banking Group won't pay any corporation tax until 2015 or after, even though it made over £2 billion in pre-tax profits. Ian Fraser writes a good summary of the analysis of Lloyds results over on 'Naked Capitalism', and the point made is that creative accounting can make any bank look good.

Lloyds was buoyant about rebounding from more than £6 billion in losses in 2009 to a £2.2 billion profit in 2010 … except that the statutory profit was a loss of £320 million.

There are many definitions of profit. Charges of £1.65 billion as the cost of integrating HBOS with Lloyds, a £500 million purse to reimburse mortgage customers for over-charging and a £365m loss on the sale of two oil-rig subsidiaries had been stripped out of the 'profit' figures.

There are many definitions of profit.

There is also a thing called "fair value unwind". In Lloyds' accounts, they have a specific area relating to the HBOS acquisition representing fair value, and the "fair value unwind represents the impact on the consolidated and divisional income statements of the acquisition related balance sheet adjustments. These adjustments principally reflect the application of market-based credit spreads to HBOS's lending portfolios and own debt."

In other words, it is the write-down of what was over-valued in the HBOS takeover and, as a result, higher valuations on HBOS assets and business lines since the deal was done had added £3.12 billion to Lloyds' headline pre-tax figure.

There are many definitions of profit.

There was a further £7.9 billion of largely unidentified 'available for sale' assets also moved into a newly-created accounting basket of 'held to maturity' assets as part of the "fair value unwind". This is a good move as such assets don't need to be marked to market, which can also improve the accounting view.

*The Extraordinary Madness of Banks and the
Extreme Folly of Governments*

There are many definitions of profit.

HSBC has faced similar questions about taxes from US authorities and UK activist groups, whilst Royal Bank of Scotland doesn't have to worry about profits right now – they made a £1.1 billion loss – but they don't have to worry about taxes either:

> "RBS finance director Bruce van Saun also admitted today the bank would pay no corporation tax again in 2011 as it has deferred tax assets of £6.3bn it can use up from previous losses before paying any tax."

All in all, this new dialogue is quite concerning as transparency in bank accounting is hard – there are differences between US and international accounting rules for example, between GAAP and IFRS, and then there are all these complexities layered on top between mark-to-market, fair value, liabilities and impairments, on balance sheet and off balance sheet, and so on and so froth.

Which finally brings me to Basel III. Basel III is a subject I generally try to avoid, but it has raised its ugly head with a report from the Matrix Group, published online by David McKibbin. Why does this report worry me? Check out the management summary:

> "We believe that changes in regulations for bank capital are a 'game changer' for the sector.
>
> The proposals from the Basel Committee published in December 2009 will increase the quantum of capital in the system, improve its quality, force out complexity from balance sheets and ultimately drive down ROE.
>
> We undertake a thorough analysis of what happens to the banks' capital in an attempt to replicate as closely as possible the anticipated findings of the Basel Committee's own impact study, due H2 2010.
>
> The results are very interesting.

132

The UK banks Lloyds and HSBC are significantly impacted by the proposals.

We see Lloyds, in particular, having a new Core Tier ratio of only 4.4% by the end of 2012.

The fall is mainly due to the full deduction from common equity of investments in other financial institutions of £10bn (mainly insurance), which under the present FSA transition rules, is only deducted at the total capital level (not 50:50 from Tier 1 and Tier 2 capital as for most other banks).

Basel III is essentially crystallising the problem that Lloyds has been able to get away with for years of double counting the capital in other financial entities on the group balance sheet.

We also see HSBC's Core Tier 1 ratio falling to 6.0%, significantly below peers and in line with what we would deem to be an appropriate regulatory minimum.

The reasons for the substantial fall in the Core Tier 1 ratio are more varied than for Lloyds and arise mainly from the deduction of negative AFS reserves, the deduction of minorities, the increase in market risk weights and the deduction of investments in other financial entities.

For the last point, HSBC has, like Lloyds, taken advantage of the FSA transition rules currently in force and opted to deduct investments in financial entities at the total capital level rather than 50:50 from Tier 1 and Tier 2 capital.

We believe that management may ultimately desire to raise more common equity to obtain a capital buffer and regain parity with peers."

Be assured that bank accounting rules are under intense scrutiny, and will be more so in the future. But no bank is going to appreciate Basel III adding layers of excess capital requirements to their already over-burdened balance sheets.

For example, take note of this quote from Karen Fawcett, Senior Managing Director and Group Head of Transaction Banking with Standard Chartered Bank:

> "If the regulations are implemented as they are currently written, we could be seeing a 2% fall in global trade and a 0.5% fall in global GDP."

What the banks are really saying is that if Basel III is implemented as it is currently written, and if banks ever move to accounting practices where apples can be compared with apples, then global trade will decrease because the lubricants of trade – leverage and risk – will be curtailed.

Is that such a bad thing?

How much have the bank bailouts cost UK taxpayers? (2011)

This was a question posed to me by Sky News, and the answer is: however much you want to report. This is based upon the fact that there are lies, darned lies and statistics, and you can manipulate the spend, exposure and loss for each taxpayer any which way you choose.

For example, the National Audit Office said that we spent £850 billion on the bank crises in 2009. That would equate to a £26,562 and fifty pence spend by every taxpayer in the UK.

Those figures are broken down into:

- ◆ £76 billion on the shares in RBS and Lloyds;
- ◆ £200 billion for liquidity support through the Bank of England (quantitative easing);
- ◆ £250 billion in guarantees on banks' borrowings;
- ◆ £40 billion in loans to Bradford & Bingley and others; and
- ◆ £280 billion in providing insurance cover for banks' assets.

134

But the £26,562.50 figure is a total exposure, not losses or actual spending.

So then we can parry this down and look specifically at figures such as the share prices of RBS and Lloyds. Again, there are different stats, e.g. £76 billion above, £65.8 billion in other news reports and £62.62 billion according to the UKFI. These figures vary as the share prices are based upon differing amounts gross versus net, with the UKFI taking the net figures in their annual report so I'll do the same (in the Sky interview I was using other stats).

According to those figures, the UK taxpayer owns £45.22 billion of RBS (83%) and £17.42 of Lloyds (41%). RBS shares were trading at 50 pence per share when the government intervened, and Lloyds were 74 pence. The shares are now 32 pence and 40 pence respectively. So you could say that the loss on paper for just these two banks is:

◆   RBS is down 34% and so the loss is £13.566 billion; and
◆   Lloyds is down 46% or just over £8 billion.

So, on paper, these two banks have lost over £21.5 billion, or around £700 for each UK taxpayer.

Then there's Northern Rock, Bradford & Bingley et al on top.

So the figures of how much this crisis has cost can vary from anything as low as £700 to over £26,500 per person. The truth is that it doesn't actually matter but, for the sake of argument, Sky News put the figure at over £3,500 per person. This is based upon:

◆   £45.22 billion in RBS shares;
◆   £17.42 billion in Lloyds shares;
◆   £27 billion in loans to Bradford & Bingley;
◆   £20.7 billion owed by Northern Rock; and
◆   £1.4 billion invested in Northern Rock's high street business.

The figures all come from the UKFI report, and work out to be £3,562 per taxpayer in exposure. Bear in mind, however, that these are not losses, but the cost to the taxpayer which may be recouped.

So you can see the lies, darned lies and statistics view of the world. I could spin the numbers to be anything from a few hundred pounds lost for each taxpayer to over £26,000 exposure for everyone.

The more important question is when will the government and taxpayer recoup these costs, if ever. As I have said before: just before the next UK general election. I'm now not so sure as, to recoup the investment made, the UKFI originally stated that the average buy-in price for Lloyds would need to be at £1.226 per share and 50.5 pence for RBS.

Hmmmm ... we are a long way from those numbers right now and the question is will they reach these levels any time soon? I originally thought yes but, with a double dip recession and other clouds on the horizon right now, it's more likely that this will be a waiting game.

A long one.

Let bad banks fail (2009)

I was invited to Ireland this week to join a debate at the University College Cork's Philosophical Debating Society. The debate was entitled 'This House believes that we should let banks go to the wall' – as in, banks should die if they are failing.

I offered to take either side of the debate, as I can argue my way out of a paper bag, and they gave me the proposing motion. My rival was Ciaran Hancock, Business Affairs Correspondent with the Irish and UK Times, who opposed the motion.

I don't have time to report the whole debate so I'm just going to present my one-sided view. Please bear in mind that I could quite easily have argued either corner, so these views are not necessarily my own.

Ladies and gentlemen:
The problem with our world today is that the banks have over-leveraged and the implosion of credit they created is now our monster to tame. For each euro a bank owned, they generated 10 or even 100 euros of debt. That debt mountain has to be eroded before the good times can roll again.

The real question therefore, is should that debt mountain be vanquished today or in years to come?

If your answer is for years to come, then support the government's actions and pump cash into the ailing system of finance. Give this debt mountain to the next generation, as in your kids.

On the other hand, if your answer is that we should swallow our medicine now in order to get over this headache, then we should allow the banks to go to the wall. At least we can then move on with a clean sheet for the future.

I vote for the latter choice because it will make us fitter for the future, rather than having a long-term pain in the rear.

All of this started back in 2002. Back then, the leverage of credit was nowhere near as horrendous as it is today. Since then, in the five years that followed, derivatives markets created around $20 trillion of false credit – money that did not exist. This was being generated in the USA and across Europe through credit derivatives, and it created a housing bubble and world of money that was non-sustainable, non-believable and non-existent.

The fall of Lehman Brothers in 2008 ended that rollercoaster ride forever, and the consequent hard landing means that we now have to pay back that $20 trillion-plus of credit.

That is the size of this correction, in fact it could be even greater, and this is why banks should be allowed to go to the wall.

*The Extraordinary Madness of Banks and the
Extreme Folly of Governments*

Banks should be allowed to go to the wall because the defenders of free market economics supported and promoted the efficient operation of markets. They actively defended the use of credit default swaps, collateralised debt obligations and other free market tools. They claimed these were just examples of the free markets at work. They cheerfully endorsed the self-regulation of the financial markets on the basis that only the fittest survive.

So why are they not supporting, promoting, cheering, endorsing and defending free market economics today?

In a free markets world, those that have fail are supposed to do just that: fail. The banks that are not the fittest should not survive. They should be allowed to go to the wall.

Why won't we let these banks fail therefore? Because they are 'too big to fail', 'too integral to our economy' or 'too important for society'?

No. Banks are not allowed to fail because politicians would lose their jobs and, as a consequence, our societies might run to anarchy.

If we were all allowed to lose our money on deposit and businesses were suddenly unable to process payments or gain access to capital, our economies would crash, unemployment would rise and riots would ensue.

We have seen this in Greece recently, and every day there is picketing outside the parliament of Iceland to show the anger and hurt their country is feeling.

This is the reality of letting banks fail and this would be the reality here in Ireland, across Europe and most countries impacted by this crisis.

But politicians losing their offices, bankers losing their jobs and society facing levels of unemployment and disruption is exactly what we have to face up to, if we are to get over this glitch.

Let me put it another way; if we do not swallow this pain today then we are just postponing it for tomorrow. By not letting banks

138

fail, we are placing the burden of their debt and our gluttony on our children and our children's children. There is the rub. So we should take our medicine today and be done with it, rather than living on our greed and letting our children and grandchildren pay for it.

And even if we do not let banks fail, we do not solve the problem. We just exacerbate it.

By not letting banks fail, governments are pumping tens of billions of dollars into a system that is broken. This system is not fixable, or appears not to be. After all, the US and European governments sank over a trillion dollars into the system in October and it is still broken. These governments came back with a further multi-trillion dollar package just this month, and it is still broken.

All that the government's actions have achieved is to realign the balance sheet of the banks and line the bankster's pockets. This purely demonstrates therefore that providing liquidity from government coffers does not work.

What about nationalising the banks then? Well, that does not work either.

By nationalising the banks all you achieve is inefficiency and imbalance. You cannot have a system where some banks are government-owned and some are not. So do we nationalise all of them, including the healthy banks, just because some rotten apples have poisoned the barrel? That is not fair.

Equally, by nationalising a few, that is also not fair. The ones that are nationalised become lazy and complacent, and they will continually be beaten by the ones that are not. Furthermore, by nationalising institutions where neither the institutions themselves nor the government wants to nationalise them, we create an even worse situation.

No, let bad banks fail and be done with it.

The Extraordinary Madness of Banks and the
Extreme Folly of Governments

And what would happen if we did let banks go to the wall? What would be the worst scenario? Riots, anarchy, revolution, civil war?

Possibly ... but only if we let all the banks fail, including the good ones. Equally, there are alternatives.

For example Joseph Stiglitz, the Nobel Prize winning economist, believes that banks should be allowed to fail. The way he would do it is to have the government guarantee and secure all depositors' monies, along with the current bank operations, buildings and branches. The government then wipes out their balance sheet debts by declaring the banks bankrupt and, through the same process, they then create new banks that are healthy. When the new banks prove to be robust, they are then returned to the private sector with a clean bill of health.

This approach has some merit, as it focuses upon creating good banks. After all, who wants to create 'bad banks'? Who wants a 'toxic bank'? What is the point of that?

Let the bad banks fail.

And let us not forget that we are not saying let all banks fail. Just the ones that are broken. There are still healthy banks out there and, in the rules of free market economics, these banks should be allowed to be more powerful and competitive at the expense of the ones that are ailing and weak. Let the fittest survive and let the weakest go to the wall.

Equally, in a world where technology is a critical component, there are many new ways of gaining access to finance anyway, with several new financial providers in play.

In the UK, we have seen several new banks being launched by local governments, the Post Office, Metro Bank and more. We have also seen new providers such as Zopa, Wonga, SmartyPig and the Barter Network, to name but a few.

There are healthy banks and alternative banks therefore who can prop up our system.

Result? If the ailing and weak banks that over-leveraged cannot cover their capital, then let them fail. Others will be left standing that are efficient and appropriate. This is how free market economics works, and I wonder why the free market economists and politicians don't get this.

In conclusion, the real reason we won't let bad banks fail is because politicians are too fearful of losing their jobs and society is too concerned about losing the good times.

But here is the core of the reason banks should be allowed to go to the wall: if we don't lose jobs and the good times now, then someone will lose them later. And that someone is you, your children and your children's children.

All we are doing is deferring the issue through stimulus packages to saddle future generations with debts and taxes. Equally, as George Osborne the UK's Shadow Chancellor, recently stated, we have allowed the capitalisation of the profits through the socialisation of the losses. Banksters enjoyed the freedom of the city in the good times whilst giving us all the hurt for the bad times.

This is wrong.

So let the systems fail, the bad banks go to the wall, the cleansing of the system and its cancerous over-leveraged poison, and create a new world order that works far better than the broken one of today.

Thank you.

My opponent then presented some thoughts about how government guarantees meant that we were not deferring taxes to future generations; how 30,000 bankers on the dole queues would not be right; that AIB and other banks had announced lending was coming back to SMEs and more; that the government could not do the job the banks do; that 100,000 people would be laid off in Ireland this year with unemployment rising to 12% of the population; that growth was down 6% this year and was only getting worse; and so on.

His bottom line was that we could not let the banks go to the wall, as all of this would just get worse and that was untenable.

We then had a long debate with the audience of students and Corkonians (no, people from Cork are not called Corkers) with comments such as the fact that Anglo-Irish Bank is a disgrace which fuelled and protected property developers and no-one else; that the government's guarantees have purely underwritten foreign business loans; that the world today is characterised by insecurity and doubt and that we need security and certainty for an economy to work; that banks fulfil a role the state does not and cannot, after all where else do business start-ups have to go other than a bank for capital; that if banks fail, we fail as a society and that our property becomes their property and we all go to the wall; and more.

Finally, we came to conclusions.

I've already outlined most of what was said but, in my concluding remarks, I did say that the issue we face today is the deleveraging of our over-leverage.

When Lehman Brothers collapsed, over $550 billion was withdrawn from the US banking system in hours. This would have led to the collapse of America within a day if action had not been taken. That incident created the fear, uncertainty and doubt (FUD) we face today, and that if we do not let more bad banks fail, we can never get back to certainty and security.

The fact that every $1 billion in losses at Lehman could equate to $20 billion or more of losses on credit default swaps created the FUD. No-one knew where or with whom these losses would occur and, with $400 billion of losses, that meant the world expected up to $10 trillion of exposure.

That was, and is, the issue.

This has resulted in the strangulation of credit and access to capital, which is why Ireland is now paying €3.50 for every €100 to insure its sovereign debt, compared with only €0.10 for every €100 just a year ago.

This is unsustainable when you have public sector debt in Ireland expected to rise by €15 billion this year alone, to €70 billion overall, and 220% of the country's annual economic output pledged to the banking system.

That is why bad banks should go to the wall. There will still be good banks, there will still be new banks, but bad banks need to go to the wall.

We then had a vote and the motion was carried … by about one vote. Banks should be allowed to go to the wall. Even with all of this emotion and reasoned argument, students and Corkonians were still split about whether banks should be allowed to fail.

But then, with lots of money in savings for the pensioners in the room and a debating society full of budding lawyers (yes, that's the core group of graduates in a debating room), it's not surprising the motion was only just carried. After all, who wants to see a bank fail when they are either providing your current or future income?

We believe banks should (not) fail? (2009)

In response to the question 'Why should banks be allowed to fail?' a friend of mine gave me three sheets of neatly written paper arguing the case. As this came from a banker, it had me worried.

So, here are 20 reasons to let banks go under:

1) To protect sovereign indebtedness – can governments truly afford to prop up the banking systems with their promises?

The Extraordinary Madness of Banks and the Extreme Folly of Governments

2) It's better to jail bankers than politicians, so let them fail and hang the bankers responsible.

3) By letting banks fail, at least you can apportion blame and punish those responsible.

4) Let the banks fail that should fail, and the markets will return to normality sooner rather than later

5) Let the banks fail, as the taxpayer will not be held responsible at least.

6) The industry has to restructure anyway so, by letting the banks fail, this can happen sooner rather than later.

7) If banking is meant to be free trade with principles based regulation, then this can draw a line to say that model is broken. The banks don't work and the state should not take a strong arm in systems that are meant to be 'free'.

8) If the USA can let Lehman fail, why should we prop up our ailing banks?

9) Let banks fail because it will accelerate reform in the industry.

10) Bonuses, compensation culture, infectious greed ... let banks fail as it will define the limits of moral hazard in these markets.

11) Let banks fail as it will allow investors to pick up the best parts of banks that were working whilst letting the bad parts rot with government.

12) Let banks fail ... who would vote for a national 'bad bank' to be created at the taxpayers' expense?

13) We need a national review of bank culture, rewards and practices and this would allow one to take place.

14) By letting banks fail, the government guarantees could be revoked and the size of the issue made known.

15) The market needs new models for lending and this would allow the markets to create them.

16) It would get rid of this idea that banks can do what they want and the state will protect them.

17) Let our banks fail as it will allow the state to adopt international standards and best practices.

18) If you let the banks fail, the government cannot be charge with cronyism (giving jobs to their banking friends).

19) Let the banks fail and the government undermines any opposition form other parties as they can show they did the 'right thing'.

20) Let banks fail as the system is so corrupt that it would create a new world order and, hopefully, a better one.

Well, there are 20 good reasons to let banks fail, and they all came from a banker!

The pros and cons of bank nationalisation (2009)

For the past year, we have watched financial institutions regularly being nationalised, part nationalised or effectively nationalised in all but name. We happily accept that this is right, as banks are 'too big to fail'.

But is it right? Is nationalisation a good or a bad thing?

Most folks who grew up under Margaret Thatcher, Ronald Reagan and the Cold War years, think that nationalisation is a swear word. They were ingrained in privatisation bids and offers, the de-nationalisation of everything that was nationalised, and the belief that free markets reign supreme. Milton Friedman was the one and only economics voice worth listening to, and businesses should be allowed to fail if they cannot compete.

The result?

AT&T was broken up, British Airways had to fly free and all public institutions were scrutinised in exact detail to see if they were really in the public interest. Public-Private Partnerships flourished, and lots of folks made a lot of money from privatisations.

Two decades later, we all wonder whether this was right.

On reflection, maybe not. We now look at 1929 and think that John Maynard Keynes was the right one, and that we should allow the word nationalisation back into our lingo.

So, in the context of financial services, is nationalisation a good or a bad thing?

In the past week alone, we have seen the nationalisation of Anglo-Irish Bank and the nationalisation in all but name of the Royal Bank of Scotland. Germany's effectively nationalised HypoReal Estate, whilst the USA has all but nationalised Citibank, Fannie Mae, Freddie Mac, AIG and the rest.

Nationalisation isn't so bad after all … but I can see a few reasons for and against such tactics so let's debate it for a minute.

Unusually, let me start with the case against nationalisation.

First, nationalised institutions are lazy and rubbish. They have no customer interest at heart, are a complete monopoly with no competition, and politicians and civil servants have no idea how to run a business. The result is that you just get big, fat, incompetent, useless operations, managed abysmally. They are happy to run like this because they lift their money directly from taxpayers' pockets and therefore have no worries about funding.

Second, nationalised institutions do nothing to move things forward. They just keep their engines running with incremental spending. The result is that there is zero innovation or creative thinking. Nationalised institutions aren't there to innovate, they're just there to operate.

Third, if nationalisation is such a good thing, then why did we tell China to stop it? In the case of China, the state-owned banks were accused for years of serving the state's interests and not the people's. China's citizens were encouraged to save and not borrow, they pooled all their monies into the state's banks which treated them like victims rather than customers, and the state moved all that money into state projects, such as railroads, farming and manufacturing.

Then, in 2001, China was told to open up the banks to competition and free market forces if they wanted to join the World Trade Agreement and start trading freely with the world. Result: China has been opening up its banking market and allowing foreigners to compete and invest. They have move from nationalised banks to privatise banks because the world's market dictate that this is the way it has to be.

It's obvious: banks owned by governments are a bad thing.

So that's the argument against nationalising banks. Let's look at the arguments for nationalisation. The banks are buggered, business is being strangled by a lack of funding, the economy is trashed, and politicians are about to be voted out of office due to the wholesale funding markets becoming drier than a desert in the summer.

Motion carried. Let's nationalise the banks.

Chapter 6 Bashing the bankers

Introduction

Every day, the press has been attacking 'greedy' bankers over bonuses and pay. This is because the banks, particularly the investment banks, pay excessive amounts to their star performers. Policymakers have tied to deal with these issues by taxing bonuses at the highest levels possible and considering placing limits on the amounts that are paid. None of these policies really work, however, as banks are experts in both avoiding taxes where possible and, if not possible, moving locations and offices to places where the tax burden is minimal. For example, when London increased taxes to 50 percent for people earning over £150,000 – which would therefore cover most investment bankers – many moved to Geneva and Hong Kong where tax rates are considerably lower. This also means that the UK government loses important income, as a banker based in Geneva or Hong Kong takes all of their earning and those of their gardeners, housekeepers, mistresses and mates with them. Therefore, the bonus issue will continue to be a media football, a policymaker's headache and a banker's focus.

40% of City workers to lose their jobs (2011)

I've recently been thinking about headcount cuts. It's always hard … and it's getting harder.

For example, I wrote in August that thousands of bank jobs were being cut, adding up to an expectation of 15,000 City jobs this year. Each job loss represents a significant loss to the economy, especially those in the City.

Based upon an average salary of £150,000 and income tax of 50%, employer national insurance of 2% and employee national insurance of 2%t, this works out at an average lost tax income per lost City job of £81,000 per year, or a total loss of about £1.3 billion in tax revenue. To put this into context, financial services workers paid a total of £18 billion income tax for the tax year 2009/10, or 15%t of the UK total, so this year's redundancies alone could lower the sector's income tax contribution by about 7%.

That doesn't include all the job losses at Lloyds Banking Group (43,000 or more job losses) and Royal Bank of Scotland (28,000 generally plus a further 5,000 just announced in the investment bank). Nor does it even look at the US figures, where Bank of America recently announced 30,000 job cuts, a similar number to those recently announced by HSBC.

In fact, every bank is cutting ... how far could it go? According to one leading light in the City, Mary Caroline Tillman – shortlisted for Woman of the Year, Head of the Global Financial Practice with headhunter firm Egon Zehnder, and formerly Managing Director and Chief Operating Officer of JP Morgan's European Advisory Business – the losses will rise to around 40% of all City jobs.

In an interview over the weekend with the Independent, Mary said the following:

> "The Masters of the Universe are facing a really tough time. The shake-out is only just beginning after the crash. There is a big consolidation still to come, which means there will be far fewer banks; a 40% cut in jobs will be the 'new normal'. This is because of the tougher regulatory environment."

A 40% job loss in the City would spell disaster. For example, the article reckons that there are about 360,000 people working in the City and some 670,000 in New York's securities industry (this does not take into account all the ancillary and related services from accountants and lawyers to bar staff and restaurants).

If 40% disappeared in London, based upon my earlier calculations, which would be 150,000+ job losses. A loss of around £13-£15 billion a year in tax revenue ... or more.

I wonder whether the government really wants this scenario therefore, and the Occupy Wall Street brethren.

Meanwhile, as the industry does go through its transformation from reckless risk to wrestled risk, it was interesting to see the change Mary sees happening in the core investment community of London.

> "The restructuring means a different kind of leader is emerging. They are coming from the more functional areas. You can see that, with risk officers such as Robert Le Blanc at Barclays and Marc Moses at HSBC, who are now at the top ... Boards want the finance guys, accountants, risk specialists, those with knowledge of IT and compliance. These are the future Masters of the Universe ... and these new bankers are determined to show that banking can be a decent and good business."

Good.

Launching the Rage Gauge (2010)

OK, it's time to build a new way of measuring anger with the banks, so today sees the launch of the Finanser's Rage Gauge.

Why do this today? Because the heat of anger on the industry varies day-by-day, month-by-month. There was shock and awe back in September 2008, then shock and anger in January 2009 as TARP and bailouts began. This increased to pure livid rage when bonuses were being paid at the end of 2009, on the back of these losses. That rage stayed for much of early 2010, but then dissipated as other things took over ... such as the 2010 World Cup.

However, it's back up to fever pitch again as the FSA publishes a report blaming no-one for the disastrous takeover of ABN AMRO by Royal Bank of Scotland.

According to journalist Ian Fraser, this is down to the FSA's own self-interests and their use of Pricewaterhouse Coopers (PwC) to sham up in the investigation:

> "I was gobsmacked this morning to discover that the Financial Services Authority, following a supposedly independent inquiry by accountancy firm PricewaterhouseCoopers, has "closed" its inquiry into Royal Bank of Scotland and exonerated the bank's entire board. I think that the regulator – which is living on borrowed time following its abject failure to regulate the finance sector in 2000-08 – will come to regret this feeble and wholly unconvincing attempt at a cover up."

I take Ian's comments seriously as he's just spent over a year investigating the demise of RBS and Sir Fred's reputation for a BBC programme to be aired in the near future.

On the other side of the pond, the Fed has just said how bailout funds were used, and that has kicked up a storm over there, especially as billions went straight into the pockets of several hedge funds:

> "The US Federal Reserve lent billions of dollars to hedge funds as part of its emergency liquidity programme during the financial crisis, data released by the central bank show. According to Fed data, $71bn of loans were made through its term asset-backed securities loan facility (Talf) mostly to non-bank institutions. They included hedge funds run by managers including FrontPoint, Magnetar, and Tricadia, many of which reaped handsome rewards from the collapse of the housing market."

Behind all of this is the rage over bonuses that never goes away as illustrated by a fascinating report published this week by the Council of International Investors on Wall Street pay and compensation. According to Paul Hodgson, the report's author: "More vigorous federal oversight of Wall Street does not appear to have changed compensation on the Street for the better."

153

Is that a problem? Absolutely, as "the lack of long-term performance measurement on Wall Street and high absolute levels of compensation likely helped to fuel excessive risk-taking."

And that is still the case today.

Not bashing bankers' bonuses but bankers' bonuses bashed (2010)

Fancy a tongue twister? Howsabout "Bankers big bonuses bashed by broadcasters but better being bashed by bank bosses"?

What's all this about? Well, Bloomberg released the latest news on bankers' bonuses this morning, and here's the league table:

Company	Compensation	Employees	Compensation per Employee
Bank of America	$26.3bn	284,169	$92,723
Citigroup	$18.64bn	258,000	$72,264
Credit Suisse	CHF11.23bn	50,500	CHF222,337
Deutsche Bank	EU9.59bn	82,504	EU116,285
Goldman Sachs	$13.72bn	35,400	$387,655
JPMorgan Chase	$21.55bn	236,810	$91,014
Morgan Stanley	$11.99bn	62,864	$190,682
UBS	CHF13.14bn	64,583	CHF203,506

Note: 1CHF:1.02US$ and 1EU:1.41US$

You may be going "wow", but take note: "While average pay per employee has dropped 0.8% this year at the eight banks, it has fallen 11% at six that focus most on trading, such as Goldman Sachs and the investment bank unit of Credit Suisse Group AG."

Survival of the richest (2010)

It's been a difficult time for City bankers, what with all the flak over bonuses and easy money after almost bankrupting the world.

The longest lasting row relates to bonuses and remunerations packages. This hit the headlines a year ago, and the argument still rumbles away. Put 'bank bonuses' into Google, for example, and over 10 MILLION results are returned.

That's 10,000,000. That's almost a quarterly bonus for an investment bank's senior executive and obviously is something that causes a lot of emotion.

Most of the emotion is the resentment that someone is getting paid squillions for doing diddly-squat. After all, it has been shown on many occasion that a monkey could get as good a result as most stockpickers, but that's not the point. The point is that the City traders who return the most profit to the bank get paid the most. And everyone who is part of a team that returns any profit will get something.

Just a million maybe. But something. And if you don't pay it, then the team leaves, lock, stock and two smoking cigars.

This culture is so ingrained that there are books about it, with my favourite being David Charters: 'At Bonus Time, No-One Can Hear You Scream'. It's a short book about "one man's quest for his annual bonus – in a world where ambition, terror, insecurity and desperate deeds are as natural as organic bread."

Yep, that describes it pretty well. The City is a cut-throat, testosterone-driven world.

But let's just look specifically at the UK issue. The banks are paying bonuses that seem excessive. The government is unpopular it is blamed for the bankers' excesses.

The government wants to therefore clamp down on any excess bonus payments.

But it can't. There's the rub. The UK cannot clamp down on bank bonuses, even with Alistair Darling's damp squib of a bonus tax, because one country cannot act on its own on this issue. Not unless they want to lose their banking industry and see it all go overseas.

Apparently no-one believes that will happen, although Boris Johnson thinks it will. Boris, the Mayor of London, claims that 9,000 bankers are likely to move out of London if there is a punitive singular UK tax regime in this space.

Equally, the *Financial Times* has discovered that many City banks and bankers are thinking about upping sticks:

> "A couple of years ago colleagues of mine would say to me how much they loved London, what a great place it was to live," says a US-born banker at a European investment bank. "Now they're tired of being here. They feel under attack.

> "Trading is the most mobile investment bank business that could be shifted abroad. And while many banks have show-off, state-of-the-art trading floors in London – such as Bank of America Merrill Lynch's at their European headquarters behind Saint Paul's Cathedral – few would have any compunction about pragmatically shifting a portion of staff to more attractive financial centres.

> "A quarter of staff could be easily relocated," says one European investment bank boss. He estimates that within six months, 5,000 to 10,000 City bankers could be shifted to another European centre such as Frankfurt or Zurich."

So what does this mean in reality? The reality is that the UK cannot unilaterally restrict bank bonuses without losing significant tax and income across the UK.

First, if 9,000 bankers leave then that is 9,000 x (salary + bonus). In reality therefore, if each banker earns an average of £2 million or so all up, it's a loss of about £20 billion to the UK economy and taxation of around £5 billion or more. That's a serious amount of income to the Treasury and commerce across Britain, and London in particular, that disappears up the spout. No wonder the *Evening Standard*'s recent poll of Londoners found that 68% of readers feel that bumper City bonuses are good for London's economy.

But it's more fundamental than this. If 9,000 bankers leave London, then it is also 9,000 x 4 jobs. Each banker supports an infrastructure across London of accountants, lawyers, cleaning staff, receptionists, security guards, catering, bars, restaurants and more. All of the support and infrastructure that services their offices and complex negotiations, in other words. So it's more like 36,000 job losses rather than 9,000.

OK, the other 27,000 aren't necessarily earning £2 million a year, but let's say they average £20,000 per year, the UK's average median salary (not London, UK).

This would mean a loss of a further £540 million in income, £100 million-plus in taxation and a further 27,000 or more on the unemployed and social security benefit numbers.

Following on from this, wherever the bankers move to will also become a major financial centre and hence other firms might follow, paving the way for a mass exodus, in worst-case scenario.

In best-case scenario, it would just mean that London loses its shine as a financial centre, which is threatened already. For example, HSBC has made moves for its CEO to relocate to Hong Kong and is listing on the Shanghai Exchange over the past few months, and many report that Shanghai will outshine London by 2019.

So all in all, the Treasury and Gordon Brown have a big challenge, and it's not a simple one, of cracking down on bonuses with a stupid media-pleasing bonus tax that, in reality, means nothing (the banks just changed 'bonus' to 'salary', and gave everyone a temporary three-month £1m pay rise).

No, this needs co-ordinated global action which is why London is working very closely with Brussels, Washington and other economic centres to try to create a joint agreement on this thorny issue. Without a joint agreement, one by the whole G20 (not just France and the UK), any action taken in London to limit bankers' bonuses will be detrimental to the Treasury, the economy and the country as a whole.

The UK banking sector contributes significantly to the UK and its economy:

◆ Employing almost half a million people with the wider financial industry employing over 1.1 million;

◆ Together with related activities (accountancy, business, computer and legal services, etc), some three million people rely on the financial industry for their jobs;

◆ Banks and financial services contribute £70 billion to the UK's national output (6.8% of GDP);

◆ Banks and financial services provide 25% of total corporation tax (£8 billion) to the UK government;

◆ The value of foreign exchange business passed through London every day is £560bn ($1 trillion).

Ending the never-ending bonus war (2010)

I'm fed up with the argument about bonuses and cannot believe it still rumbles on after a year of debate and G20 meetings. With Barclays announcing record profits last week, and therefore increased bonuses, the media latched onto this angle more than the fact that Barclays, UBS, Goldman Sachs and others demonstrates reviving markets and a recovered financial sector.

Sure, bonuses are irritating ... but only because we don't get them, the guys who do are as reliable as stockpickers as monkeys, and no-one knows how to break out of this cycle of paying millions for a job that is demanding, but no more so than many.

So here's my suggestion as to how it could be resolved.

First, set a regulatory limit on the bonus pool and the size of an individual's bonus payment.

For example, limit the bonus pool allocation to no more than 33% of the bank's full year profit after tax across all bank subsidiaries, as shareholders and capital reserves must have an equal recognition. This means that profit should be apportioned equally – one third – to each constituency. Then limit individual bonus payments to a cap of 0.1% of full year profits after tax.

For example, Barclays net profit was £9.39 billion in 2009, up from £4.38 billion a year earlier. £9.39 billion profits would create a maximum bonus to any one trader of £9.39 million. That may seem a lot, but it's been a good year and is far less than some of the current payouts. Equally, if you take Barclays profits from the year before, it would have been £4.38 million. A mere pittance compared to today's bonus culture but, if you have a level playing field, far better than today's excesses. And this is looking at a decent bank result.

Meanwhile, take a bank like Royal Bank of Scotland (RBS). The rules above would be extremely punitive for them. It doesn't necessarily outlaw any bonuses within RBS, but it does challenge the bank as to how to create a bonus pool when there is no profit.

But look at the wording. It says the bonus pool 'cannot exceed' a third of group profits, not that it must be a third. Therefore, for RBS, they can allocate bonuses. In fact, they have to in order to retain talent and remain competitive.

Nevertheless, you would want to ensure that a loss-making bank allocated bonuses that were in the best interests of the bank. As a result, the stipulation should be that the bonus plan and allocations for all banks are approved by an independent panel comprising a cross-section of the shareholders of the bank. Approval of the plan must be agreed by a majority – greater than 66 percent – of the panel, and the panel must comprise a minimum of ten investors including at least three retail investors.

159

The selection and choice of panel members must be approved by the home regulator and, whatever the panel size, a minimum of one-third must be retail shareholders rather than institutional. This should ensure a bonus pool and payout that seems agreeable to all shareholders, and therefore should also keep the regulator and media quiet.

All of the above may sound reasonable (or not), but then you have the other key question which is: how would you ensure these caps are adhered to?

After all, any government who contemplated the above would just find all of their banks moving to the Cayman Islands or Switzerland to avoid such punitive arrangements.

OK, so let's stop that one at the same time by declaring that, for a bank to operate in certain markets – especially the G20 nations – the bank must be registered in a country that has signed up to and been recognised as implementing the G20's taxation agreement.

This taxation agreement is based upon banks regulated under the new Tobin tax regime (oh yes, if you didn't think it was going to happen, it will!). From the *FT*:

> "For years, taxes on capital flows were seen as a barbarous relic of the 70s, on a par with Demis Roussos and Baked Alaska. No friend of free markets dared support the idea of US economist James Tobin, dreamed up to curb currency volatility after Bretton Woods collapsed. That's changing. Since Lord Turner, chairman of the UK's Financial Services Authority, started stirring interest in taxing financial transactions last year, politicians in Germany, France and Australia have voiced tentative approval. Now Japan, through the musings of vice-finance minister Naoki Minezaki, might just be falling in line."

So, the first thing is that the bank must be headquartered and file accounts in a recognised G20 Tobin tax location.

Second, the banks' accounts must be filed in that country and show a detailed breakdown of profits and losses using IFRS accounting, not GAAP (ouch, that might hurt).

Third, and most crucially, the bank must declare any movement of funds or debt to a location that falls outside the G20 Tobin tax coverage, such as the Cayman Islands or Costa Rica. This is to ensure that complex debt equity swaps, such as the Barclays transaction that took place last September, are registered, regulated and monitored to ensure that this is legitimate tax avoidance and not evasion.

All of the above would ensure that banks and their individuals on major bonus deals, could not just up sticks and move to a location outside the grip of the bonus rules as, if they did, they would effectively be removing themselves from the markets where they need to trade – the G20 markets.

Anyways, it may not solve or cover all the ground required – as I'm no lawyer or accountant – but at least this would be a start.

I think what's bugging everyone right now is that this crisis began in August 2007 – almost two and a half years ago – and blew up into a full blown meltdown almost 18 months ago in September 2008. So here we are, years after this all began, with bailed-out banks, angry taxpayers, a full-blown recession and all the news is of investment markets behaviours remaining unchanged.

That's what's bugging everyone ... so come on G20, pull yer finger out, get some actions started, and put an end to this never-ending bonus debate.

Bankers deserve their bonuses (2009)

I know that this will cause an argument, as I was having this very argument myself, but I cannot let the opportunity pass to report a conversation I was having about City bonuses.

161

The media have a blast every time there's a rumour of a bonus being paid in a bank, but here's the rub: bankers deserve their bonuses.

Put it in context. You go out for a meal and have great service – do you purposefully not tip the waiter or waitress, just because you happen to know that the restaurant is making losses?

You are a branch teller. You sit there every day smiling and chatting with customers, counting money, behaving honestly and doing a good job. Do you not deserve to be paid for meeting objectives, as per your job contract, even though the bank is losing money?

You're working in a bank call centre. You work really hard every day, taking abuse over the phone. You achieve all of your targets and receive the Best Call Centre Worker of the Year Award. Do you not deserve the holiday in the Canary Islands that comes with the award?

You see, what gets me, taking the examples above, is that everyone in society from the highest to the lowest, from the meekest to the mildest, from the most arrogant to the most humble, would probably agree that, given the way you are employed and rewarded, you deserve your rewards.

If you agree that you would be a Scrooge if you go to a restaurant and hotel and don't tip for good service, then surely you agree that if you employ a branch or call centre worker, and don't pay them for achieving their annual objectives, you are behaving badly too.

If you were working in an IT firm, retail store or similar operation, would you not pay staff bonuses to call centre and store workers, even if the firm as a whole made a loss? You probably would if you could.

So now we get on to the fact that we are talking about banks. Just because the bank's management and investment managers screwed up, does it really mean that every worker in a branch or call centre should be punished? Shouldn't staff be rewarded if they achieved their targets and worked honestly and hard, with dedication and conscientiousness?

So now you may be getting a little convinced that yes, some of these folks deserve their £2,000 annual reward for good service or holiday in the Canary Islands ... if you're not convinced, then why not? Surely it is the bank's management that should be punished, not the dedicated staff who worked hard for them and had no idea what a SIV, CDO, MBA, CDS and the rest was all about.

So now to the really contentious part. If a waiter in a restaurant deserves their tip, even if the restaurant is losing money; if the housekeeper in the hotel deserves the few pounds that you left for them, even though the hotel is losing money; then the call centre worker and branch teller deserve theirs. If you would reward the call centre worker in a retail business, even when the retailer is making losses, then you should reward the bank call centre worker.

So what's the difference between that, and the investment banker who made the bank £10 billion profit last year? Why should the investment banker lose his bonus of £20 million, when he achieved all of his objectives, worked hard and in a dedicated fashion?

Oh yes, because the bank is losing billions and is being bailed out by the government. Because the investment bankers are all greedy bastards, and should be flagellated in public.

Well, I'm sorry, none of that makes sense, because didn't you just agree that the call centre worker deserved their reward for achieving objectives? What's the difference between the call centre worker and the investment banker? They both worked hard and in a dedicated fashion; they both achieved their objectives; they both had an expectation that was met and even exceeded; so why are you being so mean and saying they don't deserve it?

Oh yes, because the investment banker is being paid £20 million whilst the call centre worker is being paid £2,000. So it's just a matter of scale is it?

That doesn't work then. Do you think the £2 tip versus the £2,000 reward for meeting objectives versus the £20 million bonus for producing profits should really be changed, just because you don't like the size of the last figure?

Well, the investment banker generated £10 billion in profitability for the bank, and is getting a £20 million bonus, so that's 0.2% of profit. 0.2% of profit is the banker's bonus on the profit he or she personally delivered. The call centre worker? £2,000 for achieving objectives in the call centre role that delivers … good service? Smiling customers? No profit or, at least, a profit you cannot measure?

So now you've been convinced to give someone a reward for delivering nothing but smiles, whilst arguing not to reward someone who delivered millions in profitability.

Just because the bank lost billions elsewhere wasn't their fault. Just because the bank's management is incompetent isn't their fault. Just because the bank had to be bailed out by the government with taxpayer's money isn't their fault. The fact is that they were employed to do a job and deliver specific result, which they delivered above and beyond expectations.

And, even in today's current hostile climate, if you feel a waiter or housekeeper deserves their tip, that a call centre worker in a retail business deserves their annual bonus for achieving objectives, then you also agree that a branch teller deserves their reward, as does the investment banker.

Just because the scale of these things is massively different, is no argument to deny someone their due. Just because the bank's management is incompetent, is no excuse to break someone's employment contract. And just because the taxpayer is shelling out to pay for such incompetence is no reason to go on a witch-hunt of those people who did their jobs with honesty, dedication and tenacity.

So stop whinging about bank bonuses and start focusing upon who should be made to pay.

Who's that again? Oh yes … the management.

Bankers deserve bonuses? You're an idiot! (2009)

Further to my promotion of the idea that bankers deserve their bonuses, here's the contrarian view I could have put forward.

How could you possibly agree with the idea that bankers deserve their bonuses, you schmuck? That's just darned foolish, as bankers just do not deserve their bonuses.

In fact, President Obama is ridiculous for even allowing bankers to have any payout at all, let alone $500,000-worth. If a bank is bankrupt, has had billions from the government taken from the taxpayer's pocket, then any idea of paying a banker a bonus is just mad.

Even if a bank makes money and has had no governmental support, there should be limits. For example, yesterday there was mention of an investment banker who gets a £20 million payout for making millions for the bank. Great. But where's the clause that says he has to pay that £20 million back the year after, particularly if he or she loses the bank millions. Where is it? There is no clause to get the cash back and there's the rub: bankers make silly money in the good times but, in the bad times, they just run away with it. How foolish is that?

And then you talk about breaking a job contract, but where in the employment contract does it say that when the firm is bust you still get a payout? When I worked for a firm that went into Chapter 11, where was my bonus that year? There wasn't one of course, you dolt, because the company was bankrupt. If the firm is bankrupt of course you don't get a payout, because there's no money to pay out. So why should anyone in a bank that's losing money and going bankrupt get a payout? No way, fool! If there's no profit, there's no bonus.

Equally, you make the comparison with a waiter in a restaurant or a housekeeper in a hotel, but that's pure distraction. A banker, teller or call centre worker has nothing in common with a waiter or housekeeper, because the former have a salary whilst the latter live on their tips. You cannot even relate the two together.

Similarly, you say it's just a matter of scale, but a call centre worker or teller is typically getting a few percentage points on their salary for meeting targets that include company performance, not a thousand times salary for getting lucky in having their bets payoff.

Bottom line: bankers don't deserve bonuses. If the firm is losing money, then there should be zero bonus and, even if it's making money, bonuses should be limited to some salary-related multiple, not millions for just being lucky.

That's better, and glad to get that off me chest.

Chapter 7 Solutions to the crisis – a personal view

Introduction

There are many potential solutions to this crisis. Tax banks to the hilt, limit their activities, cap their pay, inhibit their flexibility, and so on and so forth. None of these ideas particularly work and, considering activities need to be globally agreed rather than just local policies, it is hard to see how any solutions will operate that are consistent and cohesive. Within the industry there are a few co-ordinated operations and actions which may make a difference. And then there are a few ideas that are just out there for consideration. Here are a few of my own.

A Global Risk Exchange – my solution to the credit crisis (2008)

I have a solution to the credit crisis. I've labelled this my solution because:

(a) it might be rubbish;

(b) I made it up;

(c) it may be completely unworkable; and

(d) it could be very unpopular.

Therefore, I want it to be known as mine. I also want it to be known as mine because:

(a) it might be spectacular;

(b) I made it up;

(c) it could be made to work; and

(d) it might be very popular.

If it's the latter, I don't want someone else saying they made it up.

To the point, we have two problems to face immediately:

1) What do we do to get out of this mess; and

2) How to ensure we never repeat this mistake again.

Let's answer the first question: what do we do to get out of this mess? Well, here's my view, which is likely to be very unpopular among the banking community.

The fact is that we need to raise funds fast. We also need to avoid those funds solely being generated by taxpayers. We also recognise that governments cannot just generate a $700 billion amount from selling US government bonds to the Chinese. After all, why should the world's largest communist state bail out the world's largest capitalist state? By the way, as I write that line, I am trying to work out which one these days is the capitalist and which one the communist?

We need another plan which avoids taxpayer's anger and equally avoids currency degradation. Answer: take it off the thieves who stole it. This is the bit that I think would be most unpopular, but I like it.

Governments should state that all bonus payments and monies paid to investment bankers that have any association with the subprime crisis have all their assets frozen and seized by the government. This will not solve the issue, but it will appease the taxpayer.

And yes, I know that most of the funds will have already been spent or been moved overseas, but investment bankers should be accountable for these losses. Therefore, the fiscal policymakers will make it clear that any citizen who made money from toxic derivatives that led to this mess either: (a) pays it back, or (b) goes to jail for a period equivalent to one year for every million dollars missing. For Stan O'Neal that could be a very long time.

So yes, that's radical, but note that I avoided any mention of capital punishment, which George W. Bush and his cohorts must be considering. Bear in mind, that George W's home state of Texas is the one that has the most death penalties per annum!

This action would generate $5 to $10 billion in returned bonuses. That's peanuts, but boy, does it feel good.

Secondly, and also unpopular here, the US government should agree the bailout plan, but with the caveat that the banking industry will need to fund the fund from a tax on profits until it is made good. This will do nothing for bank stocks, but hey, they've tanked through the floor anyway, so what do we care? At least if it brings some stability back into the system, folks will be happier.

And both actions make us culpable and accountable for our irrational exuberance. Therefore, the industry might work harder to self-regulate itself to avoid this catastrophe ever happening again.

You may say, why punish all for the actions of the few? I suspect the government would answer: because we can and you should have gotten rid of your rotten apples before we did.

Finally, I would place an action on the treasury and regulatory players to also make them culpable and accountable. After all, they played a part in this mess. My message to them: if you ever allow any activities of this nature to remain unchecked, again, then you will be held to account. Equally, if you can demonstrate risks avoided and other miscreant ventures identified, you will be rewarded.

If the regulatory authorities missed the issues, then the key players walk … no separation agreement, no remuneration, they just walk. Oh yes, and they are named and shamed in the process, of course. I'm even tempted to say they should be personally liable for the losses they failed to avoid, but that would put anyone off applying for regulatory office, and someone's got to do it.

This may all sound far too stick and not enough carrot, far too punitive and not enough incentive, but hey, the carrots have all been eaten. The carrots are all those annual bonuses that should not have been paid. The carrots are all those regulators who made inspection checks and missed the action. The carrots are all those shareholders who took the dividends without asking where they came from.

So that's my answer to the first question: get out of this mess by bailing out the industry, but humiliating all those culpable in the process.

Now, to the second and more important question: how do we avoid repeating the mistake?

The mistake is to let complex derivatives run unchecked. SIVs, CDSs, CDOs are the same leveraged products bringing down our industry today as the toxic meltdowns of LTCM, Enron, Worldcom and Michael Milken. It's all to do with structured finance and leveraged products being sold without any understanding of the risk or repercussions.

We basically need to create a method to avoid over-leveraged risk exposures hitting the firms which trade in the markets in the future. We also need to ensure there is an effective liquidity management engine to identify and manage total liquidity movements in the markets.

So here's how I would tackle this one. I refer you to the story of Lloyd's of London, which had risks entering and leaving the markets without any tracking. Risks would leave one door and come back through another, without anyone knowing. This only came to light when global catastrophes all occurred in the same year and Lloyd's discovered the total exposure for all those risks lay within their walls. Several Lloyd's firms went bankrupt, as did their shareholders, and everyone called for blood, change and regulation.

Their solution? A data warehouse tracking system whereby everyone in the Lloyd's markets logged every risk they took on board and the counterparties involved. Each risk had a unique identifier so that every time it left and re-entered the markets, Lloyd's could see their total exposure. Soon, any over-leveraged risks could be tracked and declined, before the markets were overly weighted against the coverage, liquidity and capital available.

We need to do this in banking. For Lloyd's, it was easier as they are all in one building. For banking, it would require a concerted effort by regulators, governments, banks and insurance firms to build a Global Risk Exchange which everyone is forced to use.

The Global Risk Exchange would log every single financial instrument traded in the world, the counterparties involved, the amounts involved, the capital against those amounts to cover the risk and other base information.

Governments would underwrite the Global Risk Exchange by stating clearly that any products traded and securitised through the Exchange would be underwritten by government backing should there be any future failures in the markets. They would do this because they would be able to see a real-time global tracking system of all risks being traded worldwide through the financial markets, the capital available to cover those risks, and where risks were leaving and re-entering to create exposures.

This is critical for our future as, right now, no-one knows how much the total losses will be from this crisis. Six months ago, it was $400 billion. Last month, it was $700 billion. Today, it's $1 trillion. No-one knows what it really is. This is because the risks have been laid off globally between banks, insurance firms, corporates and other counterparties, with no total picture of the liquidity and risk exposure involved.

So my proposal is a system to track global liquidity and risk. A Global Risk Exchange. A government endorsed entity funded by the banks.

Who would operate the system? Effectively, it's a SWIFT for risk management so SWIFT or an equivalent new body could do this.

The new firm builds a global data warehousing shared service centre, funded by the banks, that allows the exchange of risk and liquidity information using standardised messages that are globally agreed, ISO-moderated and government endorsed.

172

Governments effectively state that as long as the risks for securitised products that you are trading are registered on the exchange and accepted, then the product can be traded. If not, the product is declined. The acceptance of the trade is based upon the total risk and liquidity exposures, and the fact that your entry has not triggered a red light for danger. The systems. of course, will do this at light-speed through low latency engines, so don't worry about the administration, folks.

This answers the question as to how we avoid this again, by building a global risk version of SWIFT for tracking total liquidity and risk exposures between all the organisations trading globally.

So that's my plan. Be tough with the instigators and publicly flagellate them. That will get the public back on side. Then create a SWIFT for risk through a Global Risk Exchange that all governments endorse and co-operate to ensure it works.

This is not simple, and I have not even touched on the other things that are in my head, such as how we get customers back on board trusting that banks are worth doing business with.

How do we get out of this derivatives mess? (2008)

Why have we seen such a massive breakdown in the system? What was the cause? Wherein is the real blame?

The root problem: Over-The-Counter (OTC) Derivatives. There have been so many issues with these products that it amazes me how easily these products have avoided the risk and regulatory radar.

It is not to say that all derivatives products should be banned, as they have helped to create growth and wealth. However, derivatives must no longer be allowed to trade unchecked. And therein lies the rub. OTC derivatives have been traded unchecked for far too long, and the market meltdown of the past month has been created by the idiotic usage of these products.

So how will we get out of this mess?

Well, I've already proposed that we need a Global Risk Exchange, and the Chicago Mercantile Exchange (CME) with Citadel have announced they would try and do just that for OTC derivatives, as have the Intercontinental Exchange (ICE) and the Clearing Corporation.

To resolve this, the New York Fed hosted a meeting over the weekend to work out how to agree the creation of a central counterparty for CDS contracts, in a dialogue with Eurex, NYSE Euronext, CME Group/Citadel and Intercontinental Exchange (ICE)/The Clearing Corporation. Meanwhile, the G7 issued a one-page five point plan for beating this meltdown.

This may help. It may work. Jeez, I hope it does, as we need to turn around this mess before more companies, banks, states and countries go bankrupt.

But we need more than this. After all, the five-point plan is a short-term reaction, not a long-term solution.

So here's my five-point plan, and yes, it's a radical one:

1) From Tuesday 14th October, OTC derivatives are outlawed.

2) All existing OTC derivatives are guaranteed by the G7 Ministers, and will be honoured should the contracts be activated through a credit default or other risk exposure. The method of resolution will be by the banks and fund managers involved paying all funds that are due from their commitments. However, their exposures are limited to the point at which those banks and fund managers can afford, and not allowed to rise above levels where the firm would be bankrupt. Any costs and reimbursements over and above those levels will be honoured by Treasury funding.

3) On Tuesday 14th October, a new market is opened called the ER (Electronically Regulated) Derivatives market. This market operates on the basis of a Global Risk Exchange (GRE) which will immediately be managed by the CME or ICE (toss a coin) but open to formal tender by any operator, with a final choice of operator to be selected by no later than 31st March 2009.

4) All ER derivatives can only be traded if you can prove a direct 'insurable interest' in the risks being traded. In other words, as a bank or corporation, you must be the bank or corporation that is directly involved in that bond and that risk to activate a contract. It can no longer be used for speculative purposes.

5) Any banker or fund manager discovered to be creating excessive risks in these markets through their trading strategies, and that are discovered to create market instabilities of the nature of those that we have seen in September and October 2008, will be tried under a revised Global Patriot Act. If it is proven that the individual concerned took their actions by allowing greed to overcome risk, their actions will be deemed as unpatriotic, no matter what nation or nationality they represent. The minimum sentence for such activity will be five years' incarceration with a maximum sentence of death by being hung, drawn and quartered.

That last one should put us all off ever doing this again.

How do you solve the banking crisis? (2008)

Question: How do you solve the banking crisis?
Answer: No-one knows. It's interesting to ask this question because I was asked this very question on Thursday of last week.

The question was poised in the context of the UK parliament debating the Banking Bill today in the House of Commons, and I had been asked to write a briefing paper for the debate.

My answer? We need a bank shareholder guarantee scheme to encourage confidence back into the system. This is a lengthy discussion that, rather than repeat here, appeared in the Parliamentary Brief today.

Here's a very brief summary:

> "The government's requirement that the banking system return to the lending practices of past years is flawed because it is in direct conflict with the banks' need to recapitalise. The choice is either nationalise the whole industry and continue to pump endless cash into the system, or create a bank share-holder guarantee scheme, that protects future shareholder funds invested in the UK banks. The latter is the only way to bring back shareholder confidence and allow the banks to build more tier 1 capital based upon equity reserves, rather than just cash reserves ...

> "This is a classic chicken and egg situation. The government has been feeding the chicken by giving the banks cash, but now needs to nurture the egg by focusing on the banks' balance sheets and shareholder confidence. Without the latter, we can feed the chicken as much cash as we want, but it will not make our banking system solvent. And without a shareholder guarantee scheme in UK banks, we may as well nationalise the system ...

> "A healthy banking system is critical for the economy to return to stability. The government needs the banks to return to their lending policies of past years in order to maintain consumer and business confidence. However, this is in direct conflict with the needs of the banks to reserve cash in order to recapitalise to cover their solvency requirements.

"Stock market confidence in UK banks is nowhere, as demonstrated by the 0.24 per cent take-up of the recent RBS rights issue. As a result, that rights issue cost the government a further £15bn and effectively nationalises another bank.

"Without a shareholder guarantee scheme in UK banks and specific actions that encourage shareholder confidence in the UK banking system, the government will continue to have to fund further banks' rights issue and fund recapitalisation. That path may as well be one to full nationalisation."

All well and good. I then spot that other people have been asked this question, and come up with totally different answers.

For example, in the *Evening Standard*, Jim O'Neill, Chief Economist at Goldman Sachs says that "There is one simple way out of the mess, Gordon: a state bank". Jim contends that the government needs to have its own bank to provide lending direct to business, and circumvent current banks completely. "A reliably financed lender might just be the key to the recovery from the current malaise we all want to see," he says.

Interesting. Especially as some regional councils, such as Essex and Kent are already creating their own banks to do just this.

So, state banks are the answer? Not according to David Cameron, the leader of the Conservative Party, who has announced plans to create a £50 million fund to guarantee bank loans to businesses.

Three different answers to the same question, and there's probably three hundred more out there.

However, I personally don't believe that either of the latter plans addresses the issue of banks' Tier 1 capital requirements. Whilst banks are dependent on pure cash reserves, rather than cash and equity reserves, we have a problem and neither of the latter plans address this.

*The Extraordinary Madness of Banks and the
Extreme Folly of Governments*

For example, the core issue for shareholders is that a £1 investment in a bank such as RBS or HBOS a year ago would be worth less than 10 pence today.

Until banks get shareholder confidence back in the system, we will not revive this system.